LOVE

A Guide for Prayer

by
Jacqueline Bergan
S. Marie Schwan

Take and Receive series

Saint Mary's Press
Christian Brothers Publications
Winona, Minnesota

Companion books are available in this series,
Take and Receive.
Write to: Saint Mary's Press
           Terrace Heights
           Winona, MN 55987

All scriptural excerpts are from *The Jerusalem Bible*,
Copyright © 1966, by Darton, Longman & Todd,
Limited, Doubleday & Company, Inc., used with
permission of the publisher.

Selections from *The Spiritual Exercises of St. Ignatius*,
translated by David L. Fleming, S.J., (The Institute of
Jesuit Sources, St. Louis, 1978) are reprinted with
permission.

With special thanks to our typist, S. Christine Johnson,
and to S. Doreen Charest, proofreader.

Printed in the United States of America

Printing—sixth fifth fourth third
          1993 92 91 90 89 88 87 86

ISBN 0-88489-168-2

To Leonard

—Jackie

To my Sisters

—Marie

CONTENTS

v

FOREWORD

Jesus prayed alone. At times He prayed with others too, but frequently He prayed alone. As good as it is for us to be with others in prayer, the example of Jesus suggests that it is also good, even necessary, to be alone with God and to pray in solitude.

This guide to prayer, based on the word of God, will help each of us to be alone with God and to pray in solitude. It will help us to satisfy the deep hunger and thirst we have to know and love God, and it will help us respond with grateful love to our mission from God to make all things new in Christ.

This guide to prayer is for every Christian. In that sense, it is ecumenical. Indeed, the success of the ecumenical effort depends ultimately on our prayerful openness to God's word in our hearts. May all who use this guide be blessed with that openness, and may their prayerful lives be a witness to the presence and power of God at work within them.

+Victor H. Balke
Bishop of Crookston

May 1, 1984

COVER DESIGN

For see, the winter is past
the rains are over and gone.
The flowers appear on the earth.
The season of glad songs has come,
the cooing of the turtledove
is heard in our land.   Sg. 2:11-12

"A season of glad songs **has**" begun; throughout the church is heard the murmur of prayer. Quietly, and in stillness, within the hearts of Christians everywhere winter has given way to the vitality of spring—the coming of the Spirit.

Among the heralds of spring is the return and nesting of the birds. From the days of ancient Israel even to our own times, birds have been symbolic, not only of our deep homing instincts, but also of our creative impulse, and of our desire for transcendence.

There are frequent allusions to doves throughout the scriptures. In the Song of Songs the dove announces spring; in Genesis the olive-bearing dove indicates the end of the flood (Gn. 8:11). At the Baptism of Jesus, the presence of the dove initiates a new age of the Spirit (Mk. 1:6).

The mourning dove calls:
Come then, my love . . . . for see, winter is past.
Sg. 2:10-11

The cover was designed by Donna Pierce Campbell, popular Minnesota artist, whose beauty and freshness of style mirrors the Spirit of renewal that this guide for prayer hopes to serve.

INTRODUCTION

This guide for prayer was inspired by the spiritual hunger we witnessed during the past seven years as we conducted parish days of renewal throughout northwestern Minnesota.

People shared with us their need and eagerness for guidance and support in developing a personal relationship with God. Gradually we grew in the awareness that for too long the laity has been deprived of resources that are an integral part of the tradition of spirituality within the Church.

One treasure, within this tradition, is the Spiritual Exercises of St. Ignatius. The Exercises were a response to the need of the laity in the 16th century, and have only recently been discovered anew. In the light of Vatican II, with its emphasis on scripture, interior renewal and the emergence of the laity, the Exercises have received a new relevance.

As we endeavored to adapt the pattern of the Exercises to parish days of renewal, we discovered an approach for integrating personal prayer with life circumstances that is appropriate to the needs, language and lifestyle of the laity.

This guide for prayer is the first of five volumes, each of which will provide a series of scripture passages with commentaries and suggested approaches to prayer. The theme of each volume will directly correlate with a segment of the Exercises. This first of the sequence of guides makes use of the themes present in the Principle and Foundation of the Spiritual Exercises. The themes are the affirmation of human creaturehood, indifference to all created things, and commitment. We are created in God's love, totally dependent on that love, and called to respond in freedom to praise, reverence and serve God.

Written specifically as a support for solitary prayer, the guide can also serve as a resource for faith-sharing in small groups.

The series of guides makes no claim to be the Spiritual Exercises, nor to be a commentary on them. It is an attempt to make available a means of entering into the Christocentric dynamic of conversion found in the Exercises.

In committing this approach of prayer to writing, it is our hope that more people will be able to draw nourishment from the Word of God, experience God's unique love for them, and become aware of the particular intention God holds for each of them.

Our prayer for those who use this guide is that they will be led by the Spirit of Jesus into true spiritual freedom.

> *May the God of our Lord Jesus Christ, the Father of glory, give you a spirit of wisdom and perception of what is revealed, to bring you to full knowledge of him. May he enlighten the eyes of your mind so that you can see what hope his call holds for you, what rich glories he has promised the saints will inherit and how infinitely great is the power that he has exercised for us believers.* Eph. 1:17-19

Jacqueline Bergan
S. Marie Schwan

St. Joseph the Worker, 1984

ORIENTATIONS

Lord, teach us to pray. Lk. 11:2

Prayer is our personal response to God's presence. We approach Him reverently with a listening heart. He speaks first. In prayer, we acknowledge His presence and in gratitude respond to Him in love. The focus is always on God and what He does.

The following suggestions are offered as ways of supporting and enabling attentiveness to God's word and our unique response:

A. Daily Pattern of Prayer

For each period of prayer, use the following pattern:

1. PREPARATION

+ Plan to spend at least twenty minutes to one hour in prayer daily. Though there is nothing "sacred" about sixty minutes, most people find that an hour better provides for the quieting of self, the entrance into the passage, etc.

+ The evening before, take time to read the commentary as well as the scripture passage for the following day. Just before falling asleep, recall the scripture passage.

2. STRUCTURE OF THE PRAYER PERIOD

+ Quiet yourself; be still inside and out. Relax. Breathe in deeply, hold your breath to the count of four, then exhale slowly through your mouth. Repeat several times.

+ Realize you are nothing without God; declare your dependency on Him.

+ Ask Him for the grace you want and need.

+ Read and reflect on your chosen scripture passage, using the appropriate form, e.g., meditation for poetic and non-story passages, contemplation for story/event passages, etc. See: Various Forms of Solitary Prayer, p. 2.

+ Close the prayer period with a time of conversation with Jesus and His Father. Speak and listen. Conclude with an Our Father.

3. REVIEW OF PRAYER: The review of prayer is a reflection at the conclusion of the prayer period. The purpose of the review is to heighten our awareness of how God has been present to us during the prayer period.

The review focuses primarily on the interior movements of consolation and desolation as they are revealed in our feelings of joy, peace, sadness, fear, ambivalence, anger, etc.

Often it is in the review that we become aware of how God has responded to our request for a particular grace.

Writing the review provides for personal accountability, and is a precious record of our spiritual journey. To write the review is a step toward self integration.

In the absence of a spiritual director or spiritual companion the writing helps fill the need for evaluation and clarification. If one has a spiritual director, the written review offers an excellent means of preparing to share one's prayer experience.

> Method: In a notebook or journal, after each prayer period, indicate the date and the passage. Answer each of the following questions:
> + Was there any word or phrase that particularly struck you?
> + What were your feelings? Were you peaceful? . . . loving? . . . trusting? . . . sad? . . . discouraged? . . . . What do these feelings say to you?
> + How are you more aware of God's presence?
> + Is there some point to which it would be helpful to return in your next prayer period?

B. **Various Forms of Solitary Prayer**

There are various forms of scriptural prayer. Different forms appeal to different people. Eventually, by trying various methods, we become adept at using approaches that are appropriate to particular passages and are in harmony with our personality and needs.

This guide will make use of the following forms:

1. MEDITATION: In meditation one approaches the scripture passage like

a love letter; this approach is especially helpful in praying poetic passages.

Method:

+ Read the passage slowly, aloud or in a whisper, letting the words wash over you, savoring them.
+ Stay with the words that especially catch your attention; absorb them the way the thirsty earth receives the rain.
+ Keep repeating a word or phrase, aware of the feelings that are awakened.
+ Read, and reread the passage lovingly as you would a letter from a dear friend, or as you would softly sing the chorus of a song.

2. CONTEMPLATION: In contemplation, we enter into a life event or story passage of scripture. We enter into the passage by way of imagination, making use of all our senses.

Theologians tell us that through contemplation we are able to "recall and be present at the mysteries of Christ's life." (13, p. 149)*

The Spirit of Jesus, present within us through Baptism, teaches us, just as Jesus taught the apostles. The Spirit recalls and enlivens the particular mystery into which we enter through prayer. As in the Eucharist the Risen Jesus makes present the paschal mystery, in contemplation He brings forward the particular event we are contemplating and presents Himself within that mystery.

Method:

In contemplation, one enters the story as if one were there:

+ Watch what happens; listen to what is being said.
+ Become part of the mystery; assume the role of one of the persons.
+ Look at each of the individuals; what does he/she experience? To whom does each one speak?
+ What difference does it make for my life, my family, for society, if I hear the message?

In the Gospel stories, enter into dialogue with Jesus:

+ **Be there** with Him and for Him.
+ **Want Him,** hunger for Him.
+ **Listen** to Him.

*Numbers keyed to Bibliography, pp. 123-124.

3

+ **Let Him** be for you what He wants to be.
+ **Respond to Him.** (31, pp. 5-6)

3. CENTERING PRAYER: *"In centering prayer we go beyond thought and image, beyond the senses and the rational mind to that center of our being where God is working a wonderful work."* (25, p. 18)

Centering prayer is a very simple, pure form of prayer, frequently without words; it is an opening of our hearts to the Spirit dwelling within us.

In centering prayer, we spiral down into the deepest center of ourselves. It is the point of stillness within us where we most experience being created by a loving God who is breathing us into life. To enter into centering prayer requires a recognition of our dependency on God and a surrender to His Spirit of love.

". . . the Spirit too comes to help us in our weakness . . . the Spirit expresses our plea in a way that could never be put into words . . ." (Rm. 8:26).

The Spirit of Jesus within us cries out *"Abba, Father"* (Rm. 8:15).

Method: *"Be still and know that I am God"* (Ps. 46:10).
+ Sit quietly, comfortable and relaxed.
+ Rest within your longing and desire for God.
+ Move to the center within your deepest self. This movement can be facilitated by imaging yourself slowly descending in an elevator, or walking down flights of stairs, or descending a mountain, or going down into the water, as in a deep pool.
+ In the stillness, become aware of God's presence: peacefully absorb His love.

4. MANTRA: One means of centering prayer is the use of the "mantra" or "prayer word." The mantra can be a single word or a phrase. It may be a word from scripture or one that arises spontaneously from within your heart. The word or phrase represents, for you, the fullness of God.

Variations of the mantra may include the name "Jesus" or what is known as the Jesus prayer, "Lord, Jesus Christ, Son of God, have mercy on me, a sinner."

Method: The word or phrase is repeated slowly within oneself in harmony with one's breathing. For example, the first part of the

4

Jesus prayer is said while inhaling, and the second half while exhaling.

5. MEDITATIVE READING: *"I opened my mouth; he gave me the scroll to eat and said, '. . . feed and be satisfied by the scroll I am giving you.' I ate it, and it tasted sweet as honey"* (Ez. 3:2-3).

One of the approaches to prayer is a reflective reading of scripture or other spiritual writings.

Spiritual reading is always enriching to our life of prayer. The method described below is especially supportive in times when prayer is difficult or dry.

Method: The reading is done slowly, pausing periodically to allow the words and phrases to enter within you. When a thought resonates deeply, stay with it, allowing the fullness of it to penetrate your being. Relish the word received. Respond authentically and spontaneously as in a dialogue.

6. JOURNALING: *"If you read my words, you will have some idea of the depths that I see in the mysteries of Christ"* (Eph. 3:4).

Journaling is meditative writing. When we place pen on paper, spirit and body cooperate to release our true selves.

There is a difference between journaling and keeping a journal.

To journal is to experience ourselves in a new light as expression is given to the fresh images which emerge from our subconscious. Journaling requires putting aside preconceived ideas and control.

Meditative writing is like writing a letter to one we love. Memories are recalled, convictions are clarified and affections well up within us. In writing we may discover that emotions are intensified and prolonged.

Because of this, journaling can also serve in identifying and healing hidden, suppressed emotions such as anger, fear and resentment.

Finally, journaling can give us a deeper appreciation for the written word as we encounter it in scripture.

Method: There are many variations for the use of journaling in prayer. Among them are the following:
a. writing a letter addressed to God;
b. writing a conversation between oneself and another; the other may be

5

Jesus, or another significant person. The dialogue can also be with an event, an experience or a value. For example, death, separation or wisdom receives personal attributes and is imaged as a person with whom one enters into conversation;

    c. writing an answer to a question, e.g., *"What do you want me to do for you?"* (Mk. 10:51) or *"Why are you weeping?"* (Jn. 20:15)

    d. allowing Jesus or another scripture person to "speak" to us through the pen.

    7. REPETITION: *"I will remain quietly meditating upon the point in which I have found what I desire without any eagerness to go on till I have been satisfied."* —St. Ignatius of Loyola (31, p. 110)

Repetition is the return to a previous period of prayer for the purpose of allowing the movements of God to deepen within one's heart.

Through repetitions, we fine-tune our sensitivities to God and to how He speaks in our prayer and within our life circumstances. The prayer of repetition allows for the experience of integrating who we are with who God is revealing Himself to be for us.

Repetitions are a way of honoring God's word to us in the earlier prayer period. It is recalling and pondering an earlier conversation with one we love. It is as if we say to God, "Tell me that again; what did I hear you saying?"

In this follow-up conversation or repetition we open ourselves to a healing presence that often transforms whatever sadness and confusion may have been experienced in the first prayer.

In repetitions, not only is the consolation (joy, warmth, peace) deepened, but the desolation (pain, sadness, confusion) is frequently brought to a new level of understanding and acceptance within God's plan for us.

Method: The period of prayer that we select to repeat is one in which we have experienced a significant movement of joy or sadness or confusion. It may also be a period in which nothing seemed to happen, due, perhaps, to our own lack of readiness at the time.

    + Recall the feelings of the first period of prayer.

    + Use, as a point of entry, the scene, word or feeling that was previously most significant.

    + Allow the Spirit to direct the inner movements of your heart during this time of prayer.

6

C. Spiritual Practices and Helps

1. EXAMEN OF CONSCIOUSNESS: *"Yahweh, you examine me and know me . . ."* (Ps. 139:1).

The examen of consciousness is the instrument by which we discover how God has been present to us and how we have responded to His presence through the day.

St. Ignatius believed this practice was so important that, in the event it was impossible to have a formal prayer period, he insisted that the examen would sustain one's vital link with God.

The examen of consciousness is not to be confused with an examination of conscience in which penitents are concerned with their failures. It is, rather, an exploration of how God is present within the events, circumstances, feelings of our daily lives.

What the review is to the prayer period, the examen is to our daily life. The daily discipline of an authentic practice of the examen effects the integrating balance which is essential for growth in relationship to God, to self, and to others.

The method reflects the "dynamic movement of personal love: what we always want to say to a person whom we truly love in the order in which we want to say it. . . . Thank you. . . . Help me. . . . I love you. . . . I'm sorry. . . . Be with me." (10, pp. 34-35)

> Method: The following prayer is a suggested approach to examen. The written response can be incorporated into the prayer journal.
>
> + God, my Father, I am totally dependent on you. Everything is gift from you. **All is gift.** I give you thanks and praise for the gifts of this day. . . .
> + Lord, I believe you work through and in time to reveal me to myself. Please give me an increased awareness of how you are guiding and shaping my life, as well as a more sensitive awareness of the obstacles I put in your way.
> + You have been present in my life today. Be near, now, as I reflect on:

your presence in the **events** of today . . .

your presence in the **feelings** I experienced today . . .

your **call** to me . . .

my **response** to you. . . .

+ Father, I ask your loving forgiveness and healing. The particular event of this day that I most want healed is. . . .

+ Filled with hope and a firm belief in your love and power, I entrust myself to your care, and strongly affirm. . . . (Claim the gift you most desire, most need; believe that God desires to give you that gift.)

2. FAITH-SHARING: *"Where two or three meet in my name, I shall be there with them"* (Mt. 18:20).

In the creation of community it is essential that members communicate intimately with each other about the core issues of their lives. For the Christian, this is faith sharing, and is an extension of daily solitary prayer.

A faith-sharing group is not a discussion group, nor a sensitivity session, nor a social gathering. Members do not come together to share and receive intellectual or theological insights. Nor is the purpose of faith sharing the accomplishment of some predetermined task.

The purpose of faith sharing is to listen and to be open to God as He continues to reveal Himself in the Church community represented in the small group which comes together in His name. The fruit of faith sharing is the "building up" of the Church, the Body of Christ (Eph. 4:12).

The approach to faith sharing is one of reading and reflecting together on the Word of God. Faith sharing calls us to share with each other, out of our deepest center, what it means to be a follower of Christ in our world today. To authentically enter into faith sharing is to come to know and love each other in Christ whose Spirit is the bonding force of community.

An image that faith-sharing groups may find helpful is that of a pool into which pebbles are dropped. The group gathers in a circle imaging themselves around a pool. Like a pebble being gently dropped into the water, each one offers a reflection—his/her "word" from God. In the shared silence, each offering is received. As the water ripples in concentric circles toward the outer reaches of the pool, so too this word enlarges and embraces, in love, each member of the circle.

8

Method: A group of seven to ten members gathers at a prearranged time and place.

+ The leader calls the group to prayer and invites them to some moments of silent centering, during which they pray for the presence of the Holy Spirit.
+ The leader gathers their silent prayer in an opening prayer, spontaneous or prepared.
+ One of the members reads a previously chosen scripture passage on which participants have spent some time in solitary prayer.
+ A period of silence follows each reading of the scripture.
+ The leader invites each one to share a word or phrase from the reading.
+ Another member rereads the passage; this is followed by a time of silence.
+ The leader invites those who wish, to share simply how this passage personally addresses them, e.g., challenging, comforting, inviting, etc.
+ Again the passage is read.
+ Members are invited to offer their spontaneous prayer to the Lord.
+ The leader draws the time of faith sharing to closure with a prayer, a blessing, an Our Father, or a hymn.
+ Before the group disbands, the passage for the following session is announced.

3. THE ROLE OF IMAGINATION IN PRAYER

Imagination is our power of memory and recall which makes it possible for us to enter into the experience of the past and to create the future. Through images we are able to touch the center of who we are and to surface and give life and expression to the innermost levels of our being.

The use of images is important to our psycho-spiritual development. Images simultaneously reveal multiple levels of meaning and are therefore symbolic of our deeper reality.

Through the structured use of active imagination, we release the hidden energy and potential for wholeness which is already present within us.

When active imagination is used in the context of prayer, and **with an** attitude of faith, we open ourselves to the power and mystery of God's transforming presence within us.

Because scripture is, for the most part, a collection of stories and rich in sensual imagery, the use of active imagination in praying scripture is particularly enriching.

Through imaging scripture we go beyond the truth of history to discover the truth of the mystery of God's creative word in our lives. (12, p. 76)

4. COPING WITH DISTRACTIONS

It is important not to become overly concerned or discouraged by distractions during prayer. Simply put them aside and return to your prayer material. If and when a distraction persists, it may be a call to attend prayerfully to the object of the distraction. For example, it would not be surprising if an unresolved conflict continues to surface until it has been dealt with.

Lord my God, when Your love spilled over
        into creation
                        You thought of me.
                        I am
from love   of love   for love.

Let my heart, O God, always
        recognize,
        cherish,
        and enjoy your goodness in all of creation.

Direct all that is me toward your praise.
Teach me reverence for every person, all things.
Energize me in your service.

                        Lord God
may nothing ever distract me from your
        love . . .
                neither health nor sickness
                wealth nor poverty
                honor nor dishonor
                long life nor short life.

May I never seek nor choose to be other
        than You intend or wish.   Amen.

11

Lord my God,
when your love spilled over
into creation
You thought
of
me.

PSALM 139:1-18

> *Yahweh, you examine me and know me,*
> *you know if I am standing or sitting,*
> *you read my thoughts from far away,*
> *whether I walk or lie down, you are watching,*
> *you know every detail of my conduct.*
>
> *The word is not even on my tongue,*
> *Yahweh, before you know all about it;*
> *close behind and close in front you fence me around,*
> *shielding me with your hand.*
> *Such knowledge is beyond my understanding,*
> *a height to which my mind cannot attain.*
>
> *Where could I go to escape your spirit?*
> *Where could I flee from your presence?*
> *If I climb the heavens, you are there,*
> *there too, if I lie in Sheol.*
>
> *If I flew to the point of sunrise,*
> *or westward across the sea,*
> *your hand would still be guiding me,*
> *your right hand holding me.*
>
> *If I asked darkness to cover me,*
> *and light to become night around me,*
> *that darkness would not be dark to you,*
> *night would be as light as day.*
>
> *It was you who created my inmost self,*
> *and put me together in my mother's womb;*
> *for all these mysteries I thank you;*
> *for the wonder of myself, for the wonder of your works.*

You know me through and through,
from having watched my bones take shape
when I was being formed in secret,
knitted together in the limbo of the womb.

You had scrutinized my every action,
all were recorded in your book,
my days listed and determined,
even before the first of them occurred.

God, how hard it is to grasp your thoughts!
How impossible to count them!
I could no more count them than I could the sand,
and suppose I could, you would still be with me.

COMMENTARY

Psalm 139 calls us to one of the most precious insights conceivable: the experience of ourselves as a "divine secret." (17, p. 483)

Scholars are not certain of the intent of the psalmist. The psalm may be a hymn of thanksgiving. It may even have been a defense.

Some scholars claim that it was composed by a religious leader accused of the worship of false gods.

What is obvious is that it is a consideration of God's pervasive, pursuing presence, shaped not in impersonal terms, but in concrete images drawn from the life experience of the poet.

The psalmist stands before God.

In the opening verses, he is aware of the penetrating gaze of God who knows the deepest center of the psalmist's identity.

It is the gaze of the physician, diagnostic and penetrating, probing and discerning the evasive yet death-dealing symptoms of disease.

It is the look of the mentor who perceives the hidden potential within the student before him/her and is sensitive to the inner drive of unrealized dreams.

It is the mother's contemplation of her child, the love-knowledge of a creator for that which has been formed in the embrace of love.

16

"Yahweh, you examine me and you know me."

The poet is aware of God's inescapable presence.

Like the atmospheric shield that encircles our planet, God's presence is everywhere. God shows His face in depths of despair as well as in the the heights of joy. He meets us at every crossroad, even in the dark recesses of our unfaithfulness. There is no escape.

So great a love demands total response.

"Where could I flee from your presence?"

The poet looks into his own heart, and reverently contemplates the marvel of God's creative action not only in the womb of his mother, but in his personal history. The hands of God have been active in the kneading/knitting that has "pressed, folded and stretched" (11, p. 294) him through the various stages of his life, and brought him to this moment.

SUGGESTED APPROACH TO PRAYER: GOD IN MY STORY

+ Daily prayer pattern, pages 1 and 2.

    I quiet myself and relax in the presence of God.

    I declare my dependency on God.

+ Grace:

    I ask for the gift of trust and confidence in God's love, and for a readiness to let God teach me to pray.

+ Method:

    I review my life; I write down twelve special and significant events of my life from my birth until the present time.

1. _____

2. _____

3. _____

4. _____

5. _____

6. _____

7. _____

8. _____

9. _____

10. _____

11. _____

12. _____

How has God's love been present and revealed to me at each of these times?

I focus on one special event; I remember the time and imaginatively recreate and enter into the scene of the event.

Where am I in the scene? What kind of day was it?

What did I feel? . . . joy? . . . delight? . . . or?

Who were the people involved?

I let the feelings that I experienced then be present to me now.

I pray Psalm 139. I let the words wash over me. I open myself to receive God's love. I allow His presence to enter and to fill me.

I thank God for being present within my history.

I close my prayer with an Our Father.

+ Review of Prayer:

I record in my journal the one special event I focused on and the feelings and reflections I experienced.

ISAIAH 43:1-7

But now, thus says Yahweh,
who created you, Jacob,
who formed you, Israel:

Do not be afraid, for I have redeemed you;
I have called you by your name, you are mine.
Should you pass through the sea, I will be with you;
or through rivers, they will not swallow you up.
Should you walk through fire, you will not be scorched
and the flames will not burn you.
For I am Yahweh, your God,
the Holy One of Israel, your savior.

I give Egypt for your ransom,
and exchange Cush and Seba for you.
Because you are precious in my eyes,
because you are honored and I love you.
I give men in exchange for you,
peoples in return for your life.
Do not be afraid, for I am with you.

I will bring your offspring from the east,
and gather you from the west.
To the north I will say, "Give them up,"
and to the south, "Do not hold them."
Bring back my sons from far away,
my daughters from the end of the earth,
all those who bear my name,
whom I have created for my glory,
whom I have formed, whom I have made.

COMMENTARY:

In this passage, God directly addresses his people, Israel, through the words of Isaiah, the poet/prophet.

It is helpful in reading this passage to have some sense of the historical references.

God's people carry the name of their ancestor Jacob who was given the name Israel by Yahweh. (Gn. 32:23-33)

The passage through the sea may be a reference to the saving event of the Exodus through the Reed Sea. (Ex. 14)

Strongly, yet tenderly, Yahweh speaks to his people, Jacob/Israel, reminding them of his love not only in the formation of the nation, but as a sustaining presence throughout the perils of their history.

In the passage, God directly addresses the fear of his people. In the timelessness of the Word of God, we, the new Israel, are reassured in the midst of the perils of **our** lives and **our** times.

Fire and water were, to early Israel, ever present and realistic threats. In the face of fire, there was no recourse, no help. People were at the mercy of flames as fire swept through a village, destroying every home. Never a seafaring people, they also had a deep fear of the dark mysteries of the sea.

Primordially, water and fire are symbols which are grounded deeply within our human psyche. They carry multiple levels of meaning. Paradoxically, they are representative of danger and death as well as of cleansing, of new life, power and energy. The images of fire and water engender responses of fear and anxiety, and hope.

As the Old Testament word is spoken today, in our personal lives and in society, where do we experience the "passage through the sea" and the "walk through fire"?

"Do not be afraid for I am with you."

With unerring accuracy, this passage identifies our most vulnerable weakness: fear, fear of being unloved and unlovable.

To each of us, in the throes of that fear, Yahweh says: I have called you by name . . . you are mine . . . you are precious in my eyes . . . I love you . . . I am with you.

In the center of their fear-filled experiences, the Israelite people heard the incredible word of God's reassurance; it seems to be His favorite place to speak!

SUGGESTED APPROACH TO PRAYER: LOVE LETTER FROM GOD

+ Daily prayer pattern, pages 1 and 2.

I quiet myself and relax in the presence of God.

I declare my dependency on God.

+ Grace:

I ask for a deep experience of God's care, goodness, kindness and faithfulness to me.

+ Method: Meditation, as on page 2.

The word of God is a word of love addressed to us within the difficulties and trials of our lives.

I approach Isaiah 43 as God's personal love letter to me. I allow His reassuring words to enter into my heart.

I let the words wash over me. I stay with those words or phrases that have particularly touched me.

I talk quietly to God in my own words, thanking Him for His word of love.

I close my prayer with an Our Father.

+ Review of Prayer:

I write in my journal any feelings, experiences, or insights that have come to my awareness during this prayer period.

I JOHN 4:7-8, 18-19

> *My dear people,*
> *let us love one another*
> *since love comes from God*
> *and everyone who loves is begotten by God and knows God.*
> *Anyone who fails to love can never have known God,*
> *because God is love.*
>
> *. . .*
>
> *In love there can be no fear,*
> *but fear is driven out by perfect love,*
> *because to fear is to expect punishment,*
> *and anyone who is afraid is still imperfect in love.*
> *We are to love, then,*
> *because he loved us first.*

COMMENTARY:

God is love. How easily we say it; how often we hear it. How do we penetrate a phrase that is, in so many ways, a cliche? St. John reaches out to guide us toward a greater understanding of and openness to that love.

John tells us that the origin of all love is in God and that human love is a reflection of God's love.

He assures us that God's love is a creative force, a love which has called into being all of creation—each one of us!

We are invited to receive and to return love.

God's love is an effective love. It changes us . . . our way of seeing and our way of responding.

Although we cannot see God, we can see the effectiveness of His love within the circumstances of our lives. His love becomes "visible" through an awareness of His caring for us in all those people who have loved us. It becomes visible in the realization of the many times we have been spared the consequences of our sin and foolishness.

Most of all, God's love becomes visible when we feel the dissipation of our fears and our hearts expand with love and concern for others.

Even if our personal experiences of being loved have been disappointing, there is within the core of our beings, always alive, always yearning, the Spirit of love, the Spirit of God which continues to create and to hold us in being.

God is love; He has first loved us.

SUGGESTED APPROACH TO PRAYER: WINDOW ON GOD

+ Daily prayer pattern, pages 1 and 2.

    I quiet myself and relax in the presence of God.

    I declare my dependency on God.

+ Grace:

    I ask for an experience of God's care, goodness, kindness and faithfulness to me.

+ Method:

    My image of God has been formed by experience. My life reflects the image I hold in my heart. The image is not fixed: it is ever growing toward fullness.

    I will use the "window on God" exercise on the following page to see more clearly who God is for me.

    I close with an Our Father.

+ Review of Prayer:

    I write in my journal any new awareness of how God has been a sustaining presence throughout my personal development.

God—as God was presented to me, or taught to me, when I was a child:

God—as I have come to know God through my own experience and searching:

God—as I would like to know God; God as I would like God to be; God as I would like to relate to God:

Use this space for feelings, insights, questions or resolutions that emerge from your reflection on the other three areas:

24

Adapted, with permission: Simons, JOURNAL FOR LIFE, p. 51

EXODUS 19:3-4

> *Moses then went up to God, and Yahweh called*
> *to him from the mountain, saying, "Say this*
> *to the House of Jacob, declare this to the*
> *sons of Israel, 'You yourselves have seen*
> *what I did with the Egyptians, how I carried*
> *you on eagles' wings and brought you to myself.'"*

COMMENTARY:

After three months in the desert, the Israelites came to an oasis. They pitched camp facing the mountain. From that mountain Moses and his people received an astonishing offer.

The God who led them out of slavery now offered them an invitation into a relationship of freedom. He gave them the choice to love and that choice was based on what they had experienced of His love—an unfailing faithfulness.

This faithful presence of God was experienced not only in their deliverance from the Reed Sea, but also in His caring for them in the desert.

The ancient symbol of the eagle is used to express to the Israelite people God's presence and power; He will be with them, even carrying them on the journey.

While the description of the offer may seem legalistic and formal, what God was really offering the Israelites was a love relationship. *"I will be your God and you will be my people."* This love was not unlike a marriage between a man and a woman. The contract was formal and legally binding, but the commitment was one of love. In choosing to love each other, there would be created a union of unique intimacy—a union that would sustain and support them.

Like the Israelites, we too receive this astonishing offer. Insofar as we say yes, the promise—the covenant—is fulfilled and we become God's own special possession, a priestly people, holy and consecrated.

SUGGESTED APPROACH TO PRAYER: AN ASTONISHING OFFER

+ Daily prayer pattern, pages 1 and 2.

I quiet myself and relax in the presence of God.

I declare my dependency on God.

+ Grace:

I ask for the gift of experiencing God's care, goodness, kindness and faithfulness to me.

+ Method:

"You saw with your own eyes the things I did . . . ."   (Joshua 24:7)

I reflect how, in my life history, I have been "carried" and sustained by the love I have received.

I recall the many ways in which this love was made visible, e.g., through provision for my physical needs, through supportive relationships, through the enjoyment of life and a sense of purpose.

I become aware that these gifts have been a part of God's plan for me. I allow myself to experience the security and freedom of God's particular care and choice of me.

In light of this experience of all God has done for me, I imagine and record in my journal how the contract/commitment God has offered to me might appear if written:

+   +   +

I, God, as your creator, do hereby agree to love you, ___YOUR NAME___, unconditionally. I will manifest this love within the circumstances and reality of your life.

I will support you by _____

I will nourish you _____

I will give you _____

I will _____

The conditions of this commitment have been effective from the moment of my first thought of you. This offer is exempt from ever being terminated.

Signed,

GOD

I close my prayer with an Our Father.

26

PSALM 103

Bless Yahweh, my soul,
bless his holy name, all that is in me!
Bless Yahweh, my soul,
and remember all his kindnesses:

in forgiving all your offenses,
in curing all your diseases,
in redeeming your life from the Pit,
in crowning you with love and tenderness,
in filling your years with prosperity,
in renewing your youth like an eagle's.

Yahweh, who does what is right,
is always on the side of the oppressed;
he revealed his intentions to Moses,
his prowess to the sons of Israel.

Yahweh is tender and compassionate,
slow to anger, most loving;
his indignation does not last for ever,
his resentment exists a short time only;
he never treats us, never punishes us,
as our guilt and our sins deserve.

No less than the height of heaven over earth
is the greatness of his love for those who fear him;
he takes our sins farther away
than the east is from the west.

As tenderly as a father treats his children,
so Yahweh treats those who fear him;
he knows what we are made of,
he remembers we are dust.

27

Man lasts no longer than grass,
no longer than a wild flower he lives,
one gust of wind, and he is gone,
never to be seen there again;

yet Yahweh's love for those who fear him
lasts from all eternity and for ever,
like his goodness to their children's children,
as long as they keep his covenant
and remember to obey his precepts.

Yahweh has fixed his throne in the heavens,
his empire is over all.
Bless Yahweh, all his angels,
heroes mighty to enforce his word,
attentive to his word of command.

Bless Yahweh, all his armies,
servants to enforce his will.
Bless Yahweh, all his creatures
in every part of his empire!

Bless Yahweh, my soul.

COMMENTARY:

This psalm is an Old Testament magnificat, that is, a hymn of praise and thanksgiving. In its beauty, it is an encompassing theological statement vitalized in the unique and profound depth of the personal spirituality of the psalmist.

It is liturgically expressed in song and was probably sung by an individual rather than a choir. The reference to God as King suggests that the setting was the festival of the Lord's Enthronement at the beginning of the new year.

In this psalm we have one of the clearest descriptions of an individual's relationship to God. The psalmist recounts to us how he experiences God in relationship to himself, to his people Israel, and to all of creation.

The psalm reveals to us a God who is near, yet transcendent, loving and faithful.

28

God is as near as our next breath. He is present in the healing of our brokenness, in the forgiving of our sins, and in the joy of our tender sharing with each other. Just as the molting eagle receives new feathers for flight, we, too, receive all that we need for our lives.

Standing among his own people, the psalmist recalls that God's love revealed the covenant offered through Moses on the mountain of Sinai. This covenant was one of everlasting mercy. The word used here is "hesed," the Hebrew word that embraces the fullness of a love that is totally kind, tender and compassionate. It is a love that is gift, undeserved and unconditional.

The psalmist reassures us that although we, as human creatures, are frail and live only for a brief time, the fullness of our existence is realized within the faithfulness of God's love for us. We need only to surrender ourselves in trust.

Finally, the psalmist tells us that God embraces not only us, not only all humankind, but all of creation. He is Lord of heaven and earth. May He be Lord of each human heart.

SUGGESTED APPROACH TO PRAYER: ENERGY OF LOVE

+ Daily prayer pattern, pages 1 and 2.

I quiet myself and relax in the presence of God.

I declare my dependency on God.

+ Grace:

I ask for the grace to experience God's care, goodness, kindness and faithfulness to me.

+ Method: Meditation, as on page 2.

I read the psalm slowly, several times. As I read, I breathe in the tender, kind and understanding love of God. I image the strength of this love flowing through me. Just as the arteries deliver the sustenance of life to every cell and synapse of my body, so too, God's sustaining love permeates my entire being.

I allow myself to experience the energizing refreshment that this love brings.

I close with an Our Father.

+ Review of Prayer:

I write in my journal any feelings, experiences or insights that have come to my awareness during this prayer period.

SUGGESTED APPROACH TO PRAYER:

+ Daily prayer pattern, pages 1 and 2.
    I quiet myself and relax in the presence of God.
    I declare my dependency on God.
+ Grace:
    I ask for the grace to experience God's care, goodness, kindness and
faithfulness to me
+ Method: It will be particularly helpful to read "Repetition" on page 6.
    In preparation I review my prayer by reading my journal of the past
week. I select for my repetition the period of prayer in which I was deeply moved
by joy or gratitude or awe. I proceed in the manner I did originally, focusing on
the scene, word, or feeling that was previously significant.
+ Review of Prayer:
    I write in my journal any feelings, experiences or insights that have
come to my awareness during this prayer period.

Let my heart, O God, always
recognize,
cherish,
and enjoy your goodness
in all
of
creation.

HOSEA 11:1-9

When Israel was a child I loved him,
and I called my son out of Egypt.
But the more I called to them, the further they went from me;
they have offered sacrifice to the Baals
and set their offerings smoking before the idols.
I myself taught Ephraim to walk,
I took them in my arms;
yet they have not understood that I was the one looking after them.
I led them with reins of kindness,
with leading strings of love.
I was someone who lifts an infant close against his cheek;
stooping down to him I gave him his food.
They will have to go back to Egypt,
Assyria must be their king,
because they have refused to return to me.
The sword will range through their towns,
wiping out their children,
glutting itself inside their fortresses.

My people are diseased through their disloyalty;
they call on Baal,
but he does not cure them.
Ephraim, how could I part with you?
Israel, how could I give you up?
How could I treat you like Admah,
or deal with you like Zeboiim?

My heart recoils from it,
my whole being trembles at the thought,
I will not give rein to my fierce anger,
I will not destroy Ephraim again,
for I am God, not man:

I am the Holy One in your midst
and I have no wish to destroy.

COMMENTARY:

All parents know how difficult and painful it is to discipline their children with "tough love." Our God, too, experiences pain, even agony, in allowing His wayward people to experience the harsh reality of the consequences of their unfaithfulness.

Hosea gives us a glimpse into the heart of God as he reveals God's persistent effort in establishing a love relationship with Israel. Throughout the passage, we witness the parent-like concern on the part of God and the constant resistance on the part of Israel.

In the words of Hosea we see how tenderly God nurtured Israel . . . taught him to walk, guided him, held him to His cheek. Yet, the more God called, the further Israel moved away, seeking through political alliances with Egypt and Assyria a security that can only be found in God.

God's patience is exhausted and His anger erupts! He says in effect, "Have your own way. Go to Egypt. Take the consequences!"

Parents can identify with and understand God's angry response. They can resonate with God's poignant sense of loss of and fear for His people as they are catapulted toward disaster.

"How can I part with you . . . my whole being trembles at the thought."

God's mercy prevails and even in Israel's deepest rejection of God, and though she deserves His harshest punishment, He does not cease to love her. This is a love surpassing our human understanding, a love which encompasses both judgment and hope.

Such is God's love. It is felt, not only in the sweetness of consolation, but experienced, no less, in the darkness of discipline. That darkness is, as the poet Frances Thompson says, *"the shadow of his hand outstretched caressingly."* (30, p. 60)

+ Daily prayer pattern, pages 1 and 2.

   I quiet myself and relax in the presence of God.

   I declare my dependency on God.

+ Grace:

   I ask for the grace to realize that I am totally accepted, to sense the unconditional love of the Father and the presence of God as a gift and not a threat.

+ Method: Contemplation, as on page 3.

   I recall a time when I experienced being forgiven, i.e., of being loved even when I was most resistant. In imagination, I place myself in that situation. I gently recall it in detail. I allow myself to experience the feelings that accompanied being accepted and forgiven.

   In remembering, how am I aware of God's love expressed within that human situation?

   I close my prayer with an Our Father.

+ Review of Prayer:

   I write in my journal any feelings, experiences or insights that have come to my awareness during this prayer period.

LUKE 12:4-7

> *To you my friends I say: Do not be afraid of those who kill*
> *the body and after that can do no more. I will tell you*
> *whom to fear: fear him who, after he has killed, has the*
> *power to cast into hell. Yes, I tell you, fear him. Can*
> *you not buy five sparrows for two pennies? And yet not one*
> *is forgotten in God's sight. Why, every hair on your head*
> *has been counted. There is no need to be afraid; you are*
> *worth more than hundreds of sparrows.*

COMMENTARY:

"Be not afraid."

The frequency of those words in scripture indicates the great need we all have of being reassured of God's love and care for us.

It has been said that fear is the greatest tool of the devil.

In the preceding verses Jesus has instructed His disciples about the evil of hypocrisy. Hypocrites are those who present themselves as other than they are. They need constantly to be justifying themselves and living up to a reputation.

At the root of hypocrisy is fear . . . fear of what others will say or think. It is basically a fear of being unlovable and therefore rejectable.

Jesus tells His disciples not to fear because there is a limit to the power others have over them.

Even if our hypocrisy were to buy some measure of security with others, the price of denying our true selves will·eventually plunge us into the hell of our own emptiness. God would be absent, and **that** is hell.

What we need to fear, then, is only the absence of God in our lives. To the one who has this kind of fear, Jesus says, "you are unconditionally accepted."

These words from Jesus call us to make the leap from fear to confidence, to a confidence that places our lives in the hands of a love so great that not even a sparrow, or the least anxiety, nor the shortest moment, nor one blade of grass or a hair on our head is insignificant.

SUGGESTED APPROACH TO PRAYER: A LETTER OF ENCOURAGEMENT

+ Daily prayer pattern, pages 1 and 2.

I quiet myself and relax in the presence of God.

I declare my dependency on God.

+ Grace:

I ask for the grace to realize that I am totally accepted by God, to sense the unconditional love and presence of God as a gift and not a threat.

+ Method: Meditation, as on pages 2 and 3.

I receive and prayerfully read this passage as if it were a letter from Jesus addressed personally to me.

In response to these reassuring words of Christ, allow all my inner anxieties to be dissipated and I open myself to be filled with confidence. I image the evil spirit of fear giving way to God's spirit of courage.

I close my prayer with an Our Father.

+ Review of Prayer:

I write in my journal any feelings, experiences or insights that have come to my awareness during this prayer period.

ISAIAH 49:14-16

> *For Zion was saying, "Yahweh has abandoned me,*
> *the Lord has forgotten me."*
> *Does a woman forget her baby at the breast,*
> *or fail to cherish the son of her womb?*
> *Yet even if these forget,*
> *I will never forget you.*
>
> *See, I have branded you on the palms of my hands,*
> *your ramparts are always under my eye.*

COMMENTARY:

This is one of the most touching expressions of God's love. It affirms the unbroken union of Yahweh and His people.

Upon entering a relationship, our greatest fear is always that the one who loves us will forget us. To be forgotten is to be abandoned, to be lost. It really is **not** true that it is "better to have loved and lost, than not to have loved at all." There is nothing more painful than to lose love.

We are assured of God's everlasting faithfulness in the beautiful imagery of the love of a mother for her child. When her child is grown, a mother remembers. She remembers the first word . . . the first step. In remembering, she continues to give life. Even if a mother in her human weakness would fail to remember, God will not forget.

The words of this passage were addressed to the Israelite people at a time of political upheaval and within the uncertainties of exile. They were announced as part of the promise of God's continual faithfulness. Israel needed to be comforted by these words of Isaiah.

The message of this passage knows no age. Yahweh will never abandon us, the children conceived in and born of Her creative love. There will never be any circumstance or sin that will nullify this love. God's birthing and nurturing of us continues. *"I have branded you on the palm of my hand."* We are held in God's remembering of us.

+ Daily prayer pattern, pages 1 and 2.

I quiet myself and relax in the presence of God.

I declare my dependency on God.

+ Grace:

I ask for the gift of experiencing the total acceptance of God who loves me unconditionally; I beg for a deep longing for God.

+ Method: Contemplation, as on page 3.

I image myself as a mother. (Men, do this too!)

In imagination, I move through pregnancy, birth and early years of my child. I begin with the moment when I first learn of the pregnancy . . . the first movement of life within . . . the birthing of my baby . . . the first time I hold my son/daughter . . . his/her first step . . . first word . . . .

In memory and imagination, I am aware of my maternal feelings . . . the excitement, joy, tenderness . . . .

I reread the passage. I listen to God, my mother, speak to me, her child.

I close my prayer with an Our Father.

+ Review of Prayer:

I write in my journal any feelings, experiences or insights that have come to my awareness during this prayer period.

PSALM 136   *Litany of Thanksgiving*
Alleluia!

Give thanks to Yahweh, for he is good,
  his love is everlasting!
Give thanks to the God of gods,
  his love is everlasting!
Give thanks to the Lord of lords,
  his love is everlasting!

He alone performs great marvels,
  his love is everlasting!
His wisdom made the heavens,
  his love is everlasting!
He set the earth on the waters,
  his love is everlasting!

He made the great light,
  his love is everlasting!
The sun to govern the day,
  his love is everlasting!
Moon and stars to govern the night,
  his love is everlasting!

He struck down the first-born of Egypt,
  his love is everlasting!
And brought Israel out,
  his love is everlasting!
With mighty hand and outstretched arm,
  his love is everlasting!

He split the Sea of Reeds,
  his love is everlasting!
Led Israel through the middle,
  his love is everlasting!

41

Drowned Pharaoh and his army,
    his love is everlasting!

He led his people through the wilderness,
    his love is everlasting!
He struck down mighty kings,
    his love is everlasting!

He slaughtered famous kings,
    his love is everlasting!
Sihon, king of the Amorites,
    his love is everlasting!
And Og, the king of Bashan,
    his love is everlasting!

He gave their lands as a legacy,
    his love is everlasting!
A legacy to his servant Israel,
    his love is everlasting!
He remembered us when we were down,
    his love is everlasting!
And snatched us from our oppressors,
    his love is everlasting!

He provides for all living creatures,
    his love is everlasting!
Give thanks to the God of heaven,
    his love is everlasting!

COMMENTARY:

The people are kneeling, their foreheads touching the ground, listening to the choir praise, in song, the wonders and goodness of God for His people. Over and over they raise their heads to chant the response, *"for his loving kindness endures forever."*

The Israelites have come from their fields and villages to praise their God, to give expression to the deepest impulse in the human heart.

It is the celebration of the New Year, or perhaps the opening day of the Festival of Tabernacles. The place is the inner court of the temple in Jerusalem.

It is a time of great celebration and heightened awareness; the temple is filled with the glory of God.

This image, as described in II Chronicles, chapter 7, helps us to grasp the profound significance of this psalm.

Liturgical in origin, this psalm is antiphonally constructed to provide for congregational participation.

As in a litany, the leader recites a sequence of phrases to which the congregation responds. It is, interestingly, the one psalm of the psalter that is purely liturgical throughout.

The Psalmist guides the reflection of the worshipers through a remembering of God's presence and action within their communal history. God's presence is celebrated in the memory of creation, the exodus, the entrance into the promised land, the repeated deliverances of the people, and in God's continual provision for them.

The power of this psalm is that it clearly brings to consciousness the realization that every circumstance and life event is grounded in God's mercy. Only the Hebrew word "hesed" holds the tender expansiveness and loving kindness that is God's love.

Like a heartbeat, the mantra-like phrase knits together, within God's love, the fragments of life, and in doing so, inspires wholeness and releases joy.

SUGGESTED APPROACH TO PRAYER: HIS KINDNESS FOREVER

+ Daily prayer pattern, pages 1 and 2.
> I quiet myself and relax in the presence of God.
> I declare my dependency on God.

+ Grace:
> I ask for the gift of experiencing deeply God's unconditional love as a presence that is never a threat, always supportive.

+ Method: Mantra, as on pages 4 and 5.
> There are occasions when we repeat over and over a word, a name or a phrase. In grief over the loss of a loved one, we may find ourselves repeating

43

the name of that person . . . or in love we may simply repeat the same words of love.

I quiet myself, and center in my spirit. I rest in the rhythm of God's love and my thankfulness. I repeat at comfortable intervals, the words, "His loving kindness endures forever."

I close my prayer with an Our Father.

+ Review of Prayer:

I write in my journal any feelings, experiences or insights that have come to my awareness during this prayer period.

PSALM 8

> *Yahweh, our Lord,*
> *how great your name throughout the earth!*

> *Above the heavens is your majesty chanted*
> *by the mouths of children, babes in arms.*
> *You set your stronghold firm against your foes*
> *to subdue enemies and rebels.*

> *I look up at your heavens, made by your fingers,*
> *at the moon and stars you set in place—*
> *ah, what is man that you should spare a thought for him,*
> *the son of man that you should care for him?*

> *Yet you have made him little less than a god,*
> *you have crowned him with glory and splendor,*

> *made him lord over the work of your hands,*
> *set all things under his feet.*

> *Sheep and oxen, all these,*
> *yes, wild animals too,*
> *birds in the air, fish in the sea*
> *traveling the paths of the ocean.*

> *Yahweh, our Lord,*
> *how great your name throughout the earth!*

COMMENTARY:

In Michener's novel, *Space*, we share in the fascination of the young man, John, as he gazes into the night sky, totally captivated by the complexity, vastness, and interrelatedness of the stellar display. The novel portrays not only the beauty of space but it thrusts us forward into the promise and power that space holds. The narrative revolves around the human quest for ultimate identity and meaning.

45

Who among us has not contemplated the night sky and been moved by the splendor? And who among us has not been humbled in the presence of such magnitude?

The Psalmist is brother and sister to us in our twentieth century experience.

If the Hebrew people discovered the presence of God in their history, they discovered His glory in nature. They had a unique capacity for feeling and in His psalm is expressed their awesome appreciation for nature and its creator. In the attempt to express this revelation of God, the poet feels he is reduced to childish prattle. Yet, convinced that God frequently uses the lowly for His purposes, the poet lets go of his self-conscious hesitation and sings God's praise.

The God who spun stars into space has shaped with infinite care His human creatures. As insignificant as we might experience ourselves, we are, in reality, the creation with whom He most profoundly shares Himself. He has gifted us with the power to know and to love. This inestimable gift empowers each woman and each man with the extraordinary vocation to bring all creation into His service.

The word of God launches us through prayer to a dependency on God that ordains us to holiness.

SUGGESTED APPROACH TO PRAYER: NIGHT SKY

+ Daily prayer pattern, pages 1 and 2.
    I quiet myself and relax in the presence of God.
    I declare my dependency on God.
+ Grace:
    I ask for the grace of a sense of awe and dependency before the love of God Who is so great, yet attends to me.
+ Method: Meditation, as on page 2.
    For this prayer I will treat myself to the luxury of an hour's contemplation of the stars. If this is not possible, I will, in imagination, visualize and enjoy the splendor of a night sky. I will allow myself to join in the psalmist's praise of God as he experiences himself as both loved and dependent.
    I close my prayer with an Our Father.
+ Review of Prayer:
    I write in my journal any feelings, experiences or insights that have come to my awareness during this prayer period.

46

SUGGESTED APPROACH TO PRAYER:

+ Daily prayer pattern, pages 1 and 2.
    I quiet myself and relax in the presence of God.
    I declare my dependency on God.
+ Grace:
    I ask for the grace of a sense of awe and dependency before the love of God who is so great, yet attends to me.
+ Method: It will be particularly helpful to read "Repetition," on page 6.
    In preparation, I review my prayer by reading my journal of the past week. I select for my repetition the period of prayer in which I was deeply moved by joy or gratitude or awe. I proceed in the manner I did originally, focusing on the scene, word, or feeling that was previously most significant.
+ Review of Prayer:
    I write in my journal any feelings, experiences or insights that have come to my awareness during this prayer period.

Direct all that is me/
toward
your
praise!

JEREMIAH 18:1-6

> *The word that was addressed to Jeremiah by Yahweh, "Get up and make your way down to the potter's house; there I shall let you hear what I have to say." So I went down to the potter's house; and there he was, working at the wheel. And whenever the vessel he was making came out wrong, as happens with the clay handled by potters, he would start afresh and work it into another vessel, as potters do. Then the word of Yahweh was addressed to me, "House of Israel, can not I do to you what this potter does?—it is Yahweh who speaks."*

COMMENTARY:

One of the most ancient of crafts, pottery making has been practiced for thousands of years and by the most primitive people. It sometimes provides the only evidence we have of their existence. As well as being used for practical purposes, such as food preparation and storage, pottery decoratively gave expression to the story of the people—their daily life, and celebrations, their struggles and beliefs.

Jeremiah frequently draws on common, everyday experience to illustrate to his people God's presence and action in their lives. In this passage he recalls a visit to the potter's house and tells us of the potter at work, shaping and reshaping the clay. He likens God to the potter and Israel (us) to the clay.

The quality of clay determines the beauty of the finished vessel. If the clay is impure, it will resist the intention of the artist. The prophet suggests that this is the case with Israel. Only as the clay becomes resilient in the hands of the potter does it reach its full potential.

So it is. Only in our cooperative surrender does God have the freedom to mold us in His likeness. We do not stand outside of our being created; there is a decision, a will, a choice to be made. We are partners, God and we, in the continual process of our becoming. Just as the artist and the clay have entered into a creative dynamism, God and His people have joined in the joyful experience of giving a human expression and face to the goodness of God.

> . . . for Christ plays in ten thousand places,
> Lovely in limbs, and lovely in eyes not His
> To the Father through the features of men's [people's!] faces. (4, p. 95)

SUGGESTED APPROACH TO PRAYER: IN THE POTTER'S HANDS

+ Daily prayer pattern, pages 1 and 2.

   I quiet myself and relax in the presence of God.

   I declare my dependency on God.

+ Grace:

   I ask for the gift of wonder, and a sense of my own fragileness, and dependency upon God's love.

+ Method: Contemplation, as on page 3.

   I imagine myself as clay . . . .

      What color clay am I? reddish, gray, yellow . . . ?

      What is my consistency: dry, malleable, moist . . . ?

   I see the hands of God, the Potter.

      I recall how God chose me and how He has prepared me, purified me, cleansed me of my impurities and air bubbles . . . .

      I am very attentive to the Potter. Into what kind of vessel is He shaping me? A cup . . . a vase . . . or . . . ?

      I enter into the dynamic tension of God's intention and my desire and responsiveness as my life takes shape.

      How does my vessel—I, my Self—reflect the face, the love, the creativity of God?

      I close my prayer with an Our Father.

+ Review of Prayer:

   I write in my journal any feelings, experiences or insights that have come to my awareness during this prayer period.

JOB 1:21

> Then falling to the ground he worshiped and said:

> "Naked I came from my mother's womb,
> naked I shall return.
> Yahweh gave, Yahweh has taken back.
> Blessed be the name of Yahweh!"

COMMENTARY:

This is the moment of Job's surrender. After having been stripped of the comfort and joy of his family and friendships, wrenched from his wealth and prestige, Job stands alone in the realization of his total dependency on God.

The shedding of his clothing and shaving of his head give external expression to his inner experience of nakedness and dependence.

Job acknowledges that he came **naked** from his mother's womb. He knows that it is Mother Earth who will embrace him in death, even as she embraces all the rest of creation.

Bewildered, Job in his suffering and despair continues to cling to the conviction that Yahweh is as present in the taking away as he is in the giving. It is in the midst of the glaring riddle of his life that Job abandons himself in dependency and praise, declaring, *"God gives, God has taken back. Blessed be His name."*

Traditionally, and in many cultures, these words mark the strength and courage of those who know the hands in which they ultimately rest.

In our world, confused as we are by structural and environmental collapse, threatened with possible nuclear annihilation, can we be the voice of Job?

SUGGESTED APPROACH TO PRAYER: MANTRA OF SURRENDER

+ Daily prayer pattern, pages 1 and 2.
  I quiet myself and relax in the presence of God.
  I declare my dependency on God.
+ Grace:
  I ask for the grace of wonder and a sense of my own fragileness, and dependency upon God's love.
+ Method: Mantra, as on pages 4 and 5.
  I remember a time in the past when I, like Job, felt "stripped" and emptied. I recall those times when I experienced a loss, e.g., in the death of a loved one, or through unemployment, or a ruptured relationship, or a loss of reputation, etc.
  Retrospectively I ponder how God was present in this painful experience of loss.
  I bring to my awareness the areas in which I *now* experience my "nakedness," i.e., the lack or loss of something meaningful.
  Holding this experience in my heart, I pray in the mantra form of prayer, using either of Job's prayers:
  "Naked I came from my mother's womb, naked I shall return"
  "Yahweh gave, Yahweh has taken back, Blessed be the name of Yahweh"
  The first part of the prayer is said while inhaling, the second phrase while exhaling. I let the spirit of the words fill my emptiness.
  I close my prayer with an Our Father.
+ Review of Prayer:
  I write in my journal any feelings, experiences or insights that have come to my awareness during this prayer period.

54

PSALM 104

Bless Yahweh, my soul.
Yahweh my God, how great you are!
Clothed in majesty and glory,
wrapped in a robe of light!

You stretch the heavens out like a tent,
you build your palace on the waters above;
using the clouds as your chariot,
you advance on the wings of the wind;
you use the winds as messengers
and fiery flames as servants.

You fixed the earth on its foundations,
unshakable for ever and ever;
you wrapped it with the deep as with a robe,
the waters overtopping the mountains.

At your reproof the waters took to flight,
they fled at the sound of your thunder,
cascading over the mountains, into the valleys,
down to the reservoir you made for them;
you imposed the limits they must never cross again,
or they would once more flood the land.

You set springs gushing in ravines,
running down between the mountains,
supplying water for wild animals,
attracting the thirsty wild donkeys;
near there the birds of the air make their nests
and sing among the branches.

From your palace you water the uplands
until the ground has had all that your heavens have to offer;
you make fresh grass grow for cattle

and those plants made use of by man,
for them to get food from the soil;
wine to make them cheerful,
oil to make them happy
and bread to make them strong.

The trees of Yahweh get rain enough,
those cedars of Lebanon he planted;
here the little birds build their nest
and, on the highest branches, the stork has its home.
For the wild goats there are the mountains,
in the crags rock badgers hide.

You made the moon to tell the seasons,
the sun knows when to set;
you bring darkness on, night falls,
all the forest animals come out;
savage lions roaring for their prey,
claiming their food from God.

The sun rises, they retire,
going back to lie down in their lairs,
and man goes out to work,
and to labor until dusk.
Yahweh, what variety you have created,
arranging everything so wisely!
Earth is completely full of things you have made:

among them vast expanse of ocean,
teeming with countless creatures,
creatures large and small,
with the ships going to and fro
and Leviathan whom you made to amuse you.

All creatures depend on you
to feed them throughout the year;
you provide the food they eat,

with generous hand you satisfy their hunger.

You turn your face away, they suffer,
you stop their breath, they die
and revert to dust.
You give breath, fresh life begins,
you keep renewing the world.

Glory for ever to Yahweh!
May Yahweh find joy in what he creates,
at whose glance the earth trembles,
at whose touch the mountains smoke!

I mean to sing to Yahweh all my life,
I mean to play for my God as long as I live.
May these reflections of mine give him pleasure,
as much as Yahweh gives me!
May sinners vanish from the earth
and the wicked exist no more!

Bless Yahweh, my soul.

COMMENTARY:

As you are reading this, the very breath you are inhaling is directly dependent on God's goodness and love for you. This total dependency—our dependency, the dependency of all creation—is the essence and heart of this psalm.

With beautiful words the poet weaves a picture of all creation. The tapestry of images carries us on a "journey" from the primeval waters with mythical sea dragons into the present age of our planet. God's sustaining love and power continues to create and maintain all creatures within an interdependent, interconnected life system.

As many of the psalms do, this psalm also has its literary roots in the mythology of the ancient world. The poet was familiar with the Babylonian creation myth: the destruction of the dragon of disorder so that an orderly world could emerge.

Scholars also point out that this psalm carries an Egyptian influence. It appears to reflect something of the hymn to the sun god, Aton. For the Egyptians, the sun was a symbol for God. The psalmist, however, true to his Hebraic tradition, has the sun taught by God.

Throughout the entire psalm, dependency on God is emphasized and, in the last verses, this dependency is expressed in the poet's personal reflections. Life-death are intimately contingent upon God's faithful presence and care.

> "You turn your face away, they suffer,
> You stop their breath, they die
> . . .
> You give breath, fresh life begins."

SUGGESTED APPROACH TO PRAYER: CREATIVE ENERGY

+ Daily prayer pattern, pages 1 and 2.
    I quiet myself and relax in the presence of God.
    I declare my dependency on God.
+ Grace:
    I ask for the gift of wonder and a sense of my own fragileness, and dependency upon God's love.
+ Method: Meditation, as on pages 2 and 3.
    I read the psalm slowly. I let the particular image that attracts me rise within my consciousness. I let it become distinct, and see it in detail. I use all my senses to bring it to life.
    Then, gently I enter into the image and become the wind . . . or the spring . . . or the tree . . . or one of the animals.
    I enter into the life energy of my chosen image. I see the rest of creation from within the perspective of this image.
    I rest within the creative energy of God who brought it and me forth. I let it empower me.
    I close with the prayer: Glory be to the Father, and to the Son and to the Holy Spirit; as it was in the beginning, is now and ever shall be, world without end. Amen.
+ Review of Prayer:
    I write in my journal any feelings, experiences or insights that have come to my awareness during this prayer period.

PSALM 19

> *The heavens declare the glory of God,*
> *the vault of heaven proclaims his handiwork;*
> *day discourses of it to day,*
> *night to night hands on the knowledge.*
>
> *No utterance at all, no speech,*
> *no sound that anyone can hear;*
> *yet their voice goes out through all the earth,*
> *and their message to the ends of the world.*
>
> *High above, he pitched a tent for the sun,*
> *who comes out of his pavilion like a bridegroom,*
> *exulting like a hero to run his race.*
>
> *He has his rising on the edge of heaven,*
> *the end of his course is its furthest edge,*
> *and nothing can escape his heat.*
>
> > *The Law of Yahweh is perfect,*
> > *new life for the soul;*
> > *the decree of Yahweh is trustworthy,*
> > *wisdom for the simple.*
> >
> > *The precepts of Yahweh are upright,*
> > *joy for the heart;*
> > *the commandment of Yahweh is clear,*
> > *light for the eyes.*
> >
> > *The fear of Yahweh is pure,*
> > *lasting for ever;*
> > *the judgments of Yahweh are true,*
> > *righteous, every one,*
> >
> > *more desirable than gold,*
> > *even than the finest gold;*

his words are sweeter than honey,
    even than honey that drips from the comb.

Thus your servant is formed by them,
    observance brings great reward.
But who can detect his own failings?
    Wash out my hidden faults.

And from pride preserve your servant,
    never let it dominate me.
So shall I be above reproach,
    free from grave sin.

May the words of my mouth always find favor,
    and the whispering of my heart,
In your presence, Yahweh,
    my Rock, my Redeemer!

COMMENTARY:

Imagine yourself as just having arrived in a strange country. You don't know the language so you cannot ask for directions or read the signs and you do not understand the words others are attempting to say to you. You feel frustrated and lost.

Through persistence, you eventually arrive at your hotel room. Upon reflection, you realize that a communication occurred which was not dependent upon the spoken word. Communication took place through a jumble of expressions: smiles, shrugs, pointing, frowns. Through it all you felt not only frustrated, but somehow welcomed, directed, understood, and released in a shared humor over the situation. You even felt a small measure of security!

This example demonstrates that language is not limited to the spoken or written word. In Psalm 19, the poet shows us that neither is the revelation of God limited to the spoken word.

Creation is an expression of God's love for us. Nature is God's "word" to us, and it is a word we can all understand. This "word of love" is available to all regardless of nationality, education, position or status.

Nature is a universal language. Nature is a tangible reality of God's love. It speaks to us. Listening to nature, we discover a welcoming of our deepest self, a sense of direction, a release from self preoccupation and a growing awareness that we have a significant contribution to make within God's plan of love.

With verse 7, the poem addresses the law of God. For the Hebrews, law or Torah refers not to isolated rules or prescriptions but to the invitation of God to His people as revealed in the stories of the first five books of the Old Testament. The stories are of creation, sin, healing and God's special choice/election of the Hebrew people.

The stories reveal God's law as a declaration of His love.

Within our own stories—our creation, our sin, our healing and God's special choice of us—God continues to speak His word/law of love.

When we embrace the reality of our total selves—our strengths and our weaknesses, our light and our darkness, we enter into a deeper reality of wholeness. When we are one with ourselves, we are one with our creator and with all things created.

Only in such surrender is true joy realized and glory given to God.

SUGGESTED APPROACH TO PRAYER: A ROSE

+ Daily prayer pattern, pages 1 and 2.
    I quiet myself and relax in the presence of God.
    I declare my dependency on God.
+ Grace:
    I ask for the gift of wonder and awe, and a sense of my own fragileness and dependency upon God's love.
+ Method: Contemplation, as on page 3.
    "Imagine a rosebush: roots, stem, leaves, and on top, a rosebud. The rosebud is closed, and enveloped by its green sepals. Take your time in visualizing all the details clearly.

    "Now imagine that the sepals start to open, turn back, and reveal the petals inside—tender, delicate, still closed.

    "Now the petals themselves slowly begin to open. As they do so, you become aware of a blossoming also occurring in the depths of your being. You feel that something in you is opening and coming to light.

"As you keep visualizing the rose, you feel that its rhythm is your rhythm, its opening is your opening. You keep watching the rose as it opens up to the light and the air, as it reveals itself in all its beauty.

"You smell its perfume and absorb it into your being.

"Now gaze into the very center of the rose, where its life is most intense. Let an image emerge from there. This image will represent what is most beautiful, most meaningful, most creative that wants to come to light in your life right now. It can be an image of absolutely anything. Just let it emerge spontaneously, without forcing or thinking.

"Now stay with this image for some time, and absorb its quality.

"The image may have a message for you—a verbal or a nonverbal message. Be receptive to it." (Used with permission. 14, pp. 132-133)

If *"the heavens declare the glory of God,"* so, too, does each fragment of creation, . . . so does a rose. At the end of the prayer period, let the rose within you pray the psalm.

I close my prayer with an Our Father.

+ Review of Prayer:

I write in my journal any feelings, experiences or insights that have come to my awareness during this prayer period.

On the evening before, prepare for prayer by reading the following:

COMMENTARY:

"Who is this with his empty headed words?" This is God's sarcastic greeting to Job in chapters 38 and 39.

Imagine Job. He has lost everything: his health, his family and his security. The attempt of his friends to help him has ended in creating greater confusion.

Job is a devout man, yet he is tormented by his anger and rage. He realizes that not only his life but the lives of those he knows and loves are broken and sometimes filled with despair. He demands that God explain and justify the human situation of suffering and limitation that is Job's experience.

Job asks: "Why me?" . . . "What kind of God are you?"

We can identify with the anguish of Job. Do we not at times cry out with the same question? Even if we have not lost everything, there are times when something very central to our lives collapses. It may be the death of one we love, or a personal disillusionment.

"Why me? . . . What kind of God are you to let this happen?"

And God says to us: "Who is this with his/her empty headed words?"

It is God's turn to ask the questions. He tells Job to "brace" himself.

God does not spare Job. He puts to Job a series of questions about nature and who controls the world. The questions are utterly unanswerable and have a sharpness or irony and are taunting. The questions put Job's dilemma into perspective.

In effect, God says to Job: "Who are you to question me or my ways?" Who is the creator here and who is the creature?

Is not this the question we hear addressed to us?

+ Daily prayer pattern, pages 1 and 2.

    I quiet myself and relax in the presence of God.

    I declare my dependency on God.

+ Grace:

    I ask for the grace of wonder and awe, and a sense of my fragileness, and dependency upon God's love.

+ Method: Meditative Reading as on pages 4 and 5.

    I enter into the mind and heart of Job and allow myself to taste of his confusion. I slowly read chapters 38 and 39 of the book of Job. I pause periodically to allow the words and phrases to resonate within the realm of my own experience. I respond to God from the depths of my own search and longing.

    I close with an Our Father.

+ Review of Prayer:

    I write in my journal any feelings, experiences or insights that have come to my awareness during this prayer period.

SUGGESTED APPROACH TO PRAYER:

+ Daily prayer pattern, pages 1 and 2.

     I quiet myself and relax in the presence of God.

     I declare my dependency on God.

+ Grace:

     I ask for the grace of wonder and awe before the mystery of God's creative love and my dependency.

+ Method: Repetition, as on page 6.

     In preparation, I review my prayer by reading my journal of the past week. I select for my repetition the period of prayer in which I was most deeply moved by joy or gratitude or awe, or perhaps a passage that did not seem to touch me at all. I proceed in the manner I did originally, opening my heart to this word of God.

+ Review of Prayer:

     I write in my journal any feelings, experiences or insights that have come to my awareness during this prayer period. I am particularly aware of how God may be gifting me with the grace I have been requesting.

Lord God
    may nothing
    ever
    distract me
    from
    your
    love.

ROMANS 9:20-21

> *But what right have you, a human being, to cross-*
> *examine God? The pot has no right to say to the*
> *potter, "Why did you make me this shape?" Surely*
> *the potter can do what he likes with the clay. It*
> *is surely for him to decide whether he will use a*
> *particular lump of clay to make a special pot or*
> *an ordinary one.*

COMMENTARY:

Imagine yourself as a pot sitting on a shelf in a potter's studio. You have been on this shelf for a long time, but you never really looked at the other pottery. This morning you find yourself looking at the others in a new way, as if for the first time.

You immediately become aware of an exquisite pot on the second shelf. It is of perfect proportions and has been shaped of the finest white clay. It appears to be flawless.

In the corner you spot a small misshapen pot and wonder why the potter hasn't discarded it. It does not seem to have any redeeming qualities.

You look at both and wonder at the striking contrast. Then you look at yourself and discover suddenly that you are somewhat broken. You hadn't noticed it before, but now, as you look closely, you see a hairline crack that extends the entire length of yourself.

You experience panic. You question your inherent value and usefulness. Will you be able to hold anything?

You feel jealous of the perfect pot. Why did the potter fail you? Was he sick the day he created you? Didn't he care?

You remember the potter. You see again his gentle face, his loving eyes, his slender deft fingers as he selects, kneads and shapes each lump of clay. You have watched him for years from your position on the shelf. You know, in your heart, that never has he created unlovingly. Always he has "in-formed" the clay with his very own spirit.

No less love has been present for the misshapen than for the flawless creations.

You know that you do not at this moment understand why one is perfect while another is not. What purpose do the differences serve? Perhaps you will discover your service as a broken pot. You know somehow that your value does not rest in your own degree of perfection.

For now it is enough to know that you have been created, in love . . . of love . . . for love.

SUGGESTED APPROACH TO PRAYER: LETTING GO

+ Daily prayer pattern, pages 1 and 2.
    I quiet myself and relax in the presence of God.
    I declare my dependency on God.
+ Grace:
    I ask for the grace of freedom, i.e., for a readiness to respond with a clear "yes" to whatever I am called to by God.
+ Method: Contemplation, as on page 3.
    I read the commentary slowly. I image myself as the pot just discovering its brokenness. I ask myself the same questions as the pot asked itself.
    I conclude my prayer with an expression of my desire to freely submit myself to God's ongoing creation, and his purpose, for me.
    Out of this stance of surrender, I pray the Our Father.
+ Review of Prayer:
    I write in my journal any feelings, experiences or insights that have come to my awareness during this prayer period.

EXODUS 3:1-6

> *Moses was looking after the flock of Jethro, his father-in-law,*
> *priest of Midian. He led his flock to the far side of the*
> *wilderness and came to Horeb, the mountain of God. There the*
> *angel of Yahweh appeared to him in the shape of a flame of*
> *fire, coming from the middle of a bush. Moses looked; there*
> *was the bush blazing but it was not being burned up. "I must*
> *go and look at this strange sight," Moses said, "and see why*
> *the bush is not burned." Now Yahweh saw him go forward to look,*
> *and God called to him from the middle of the bush. "Moses,*
> *Moses!" he said. "Here I am," he answered. "Come no nearer,"*
> *he said. "Take off your shoes, for the place on which you*
> *stand is holy ground. I am the God of your father," he said,*
> *"the God of Abraham, the God of Isaac and the God of Jacob."*
> *At this Moses covered his face, afraid to look at God.*

COMMENTARY:

Moses is in the wilderness. His history, like his heart, is full of conflict. He is well established in Midian, but does not feel at home there. His inner feelings of alienation are reflected in the name he gave his newborn son, Gershom, which means, "I am a stranger in a foreign land."

The experience of alienation that Moses knows is one with which many of us can identify. His conflict is between who he is and who he seems to be.

He finds himself in a land totally unlike Egypt, the land of his birth, from which he had to escape. He is separated not only from the Egyptian court in which he grew to manhood, but from his Hebrew roots. He was rescued as a Hebrew baby from the water by an Egyptian woman who raised him as her son.

Who is he? Where is his home?

Mercifully, his enforced solitude as a shepherd does not allow him to escape the issue. His heart burns with the question.

It is a flame that burns without consuming. Within the center of the fire

Moses hears his name. He knows that he is on holy ground.

At the foot of the mountain, before the burning bush of his conscience, he opens himself to God's presence. "Here I am."

In the moment of Moses' total surrender, God extends a total embrace.

In that embrace Moses is welcomed **home**, a home that is at once God and, at the same moment, Moses.

Encountered with such love, Moses is overwhelmed. This showing forth of God's presence, his "face," is nearly too much for Moses.

SUGGESTED APPROACH TO PRAYER: BEFORE THE BURNING BUSH

+ Daily prayer pattern, pages 1 and 2.

   I quiet myself and relax in the presence of God.

   I declare my dependency on God.

+ Grace:

   I ask for the grace of freedom, i.e., for a readiness to respond with a clear "yes" to whatever I am called to by God.

+ Method: Contemplation, as on page 3.

   I image myself as Moses. I allow the homelessness, the isolation that was his suffering to become one with my own experience of aloneness.

   I become aware that my questions of identity and purpose are not unlike those of Moses.

   I join with Moses in the encountering of the burning bush. I gaze into the fire. I visualize the brightness and feel the intense heat. I hear the crackling of the flames as they leap about the branches without consuming them.

   Do I have within me the freedom to respond to God as Moses did, with "here I am, Lord"?

   I close my prayer with the Our Father.

+ Review of Prayer:

   I write in my journal any feelings, experiences or insights that have come to my awareness during this prayer period.

GENESIS 22:1-18

It happened some time later that God put Abraham to the test. "Abraham, Abraham," he called. "Here I am," he replied. "Take your son," God said, "your only child Isaac, whom you love, and go to the land of Moriah. There you shall offer him as a burnt offering, on a mountain I will point out to you."

Rising early next morning Abraham saddled his ass and took with him two of his servants and his son Isaac. He chopped wood for the burnt offering and started on his journey to the place God had pointed out to him. On the third day Abraham looked up and saw the place in the distance. Then Abraham said to his servants, "Stay here with the donkey. The boy and I will go over there; we will worship and come back to you."

Abraham took the wood for the burnt offering, loaded it on Isaac, and carried in his own hands the fire and the knife. Then the two of them set out together. Isaac spoke to his father Abraham, "Father," he said. "Yes, my son," he replied. "Look," he said, "here are the fire and the wood, but where is the lamb for the burnt offering?" Abraham answered, "My son, God himself will provide the lamb for the burnt offering." Then the two of them went on together.

When they arrived at the place God had pointed out to him, Abraham built an altar there, and arranged the wood. Then he bound his son Isaac and put him on the altar on top of the wood. Abraham stretched out his hand and seized the knife to kill his son.

But the angel of Yahweh called to him from heaven, "Abraham, Abraham," he said. "I am here," he replied. "Do not raise your hand against the boy," the angel said. "Do not harm him, for now I know you fear God. You have not refused me your son, your only son."

Then looking up, Abraham saw a ram caught by its horns in a bush. Abraham took the ram and offered it as a burnt offering in place of his son. Abraham called this place, "Yahweh provides," and hence the saying today: On the mountain Yahweh provides.

The angel of Yahweh called Abraham a second time from heaven, "I swear by my own self—it is Yahweh who speaks—because you have done this, because you have not refused me your son, your only son, I will shower blessings on you. I will make your descendants as many as the stars of heaven and the grains of sand on the sea-shore. Your descendants shall gain possession of the gates of their enemies. All the nations of the earth shall bless themselves by your descendants, as a reward for your obedience.

COMMENTARY:

We see a very old man slowly and laboriously walking up a mountain path. His eyes are taut with unshed tears, and are fixed to the ground as if he does not dare to look up. He carries a small black firebox which contains live coals, and in his belt we see a knife.

Walking beside the man, in silence, is a young boy. On his shoulders he carries a heavy bundle of wood. The wood is so heavy and awkward that he walks unsteadily, almost losing his balance. On his face there is an expression of confusion and fear. Every few steps he looks at his father in an attempt to discover why they are doing what they are doing.

It is Abraham with his son Isaac.

Abraham and Sarah had given up the hope of ever bearing a child, but through the mercy and goodness of God, the seemingly impossible happened. They conceived in their old age. Like other couples who give birth to a child in their later years, they, too, experienced delight of the "late arrival."

There was an added dimension of joy for Abraham. In a special way, Isaac held, for Abraham, the promise of the future. He deeply believed that Isaac was meant by God to be the link, the continuation of what God had initiated in Abraham, that is, the creation of a people formed and bonded in God's love.

Now God asks Abraham to kill this child.

74

Everything in Abraham questions this directive. His whole being reels under the impact of the paradox. God had sent Isaac. Now he demands his death, and at the hand of Abraham.

Abraham is at a crossroads; he is facing the ultimate test.

Does he have the courage to surrender to God's demand, to accept the dark unknowing, and thereby let go of all his own preconceived, rational assumptions?

It is unfortunate that this story is usually limited by being presented as an illustration of Abraham's obedience or as a statement against child sacrifice which was common in the time of Abraham.

The story of Abraham and Isaac is particularly significant in that it contains a profound personal experience which serves as a paradigm or model for the leap from the known to the unknown, the "let go" experience that is at the heart of adult self-appropriation and commitment.

The object of the story is not that God rushed in at the last moment to save Isaac and things resumed to their previous status. No, everything changed. Abraham was different; Isaac was different.

In yielding all, Abraham and Isaac set into motion the human journey toward holiness and wholeness—Christogenesis!

As we look at Isaac, beloved by this father, struggling with the weight of the wood, can we see Jesus? (John 19:17)

SUGGESTED APPROACH TO PRAYER: CHOICE IN FREEDOM

+ Daily prayer pattern, pages 1 and 2.

    I quiet myself and relax in the presence of God.

    I declare my dependency on God.

+ Grace:

    I ask for the grace of freedom, i.e., for a readiness to respond with a clear "yes" to whatever I am called to by God.

+ Method: Contemplation, as on page 3.

    I image myself as Abraham responding to God's directive. I imagine the story in great detail, using all my senses to enter within the drama.

    I am particularly aware of the inner turmoil at the moment of decision. What is *my response?*

Am *I* able to surrender, in trust, to God's directive to *me*?

I close my prayer with an Our Father.

+ Review of Prayer:

I write in my journal any feelings, experiences or insights that have come to my awareness during this prayer period.

PHILIPPIANS 3:7-11

> *But because of Christ, I have come to consider all these*
> *advantages that I had as disadvantages. Not only that,*
> *but I believe nothing can happen that will outweigh the*
> *supreme advantage of knowing Christ Jesus my Lord. For*
> *him I have accepted the loss of everything, and I look*
> *on everything as so much rubbish if only I can have*
> *Christ and be given a place in him. I am no longer trying*
> *for perfection by my own efforts, the perfection that*
> *comes from the law, but I want only the perfection that*
> *comes through faith in Christ, and is from God and based*
> *on faith. All I want to know is Christ and the power of*
> *his resurrection and to share his sufferings by reproducing*
> *the pattern of his death.*

COMMENTARY:

Bring to mind and heart an intimately freeing relationship of love . . . your husband/wife, or friend. How did the relationship come about? What were the surprises? How would you describe your loved one?

Are you satisfied to describe him/her with factual information such as the place and date of birth, or do you find yourself without adequate words to express what your heart knows of the other?

Our human experience of love is the context within which we discover how to love Christ. We experience deep levels of intimacy in our human relationships, and amazingly, we are offered the possibility of deep intimacy with Christ.

Just as our love relationships occur as gift, and never as a result of our own manipulative efforts, so, too, the love of Christ is always gift. Through Paul's story, we are assured that in the acceptance of this intimate relationship of Christ's love, we will be released from the compulsiveness and rigidity that bind us.

Fullness/wholeness comes in the receiving of love offered. The degree to which we open ourselves to receive it parallels our freedom.

In Philippians, chapter 3, Paul shares his personal relationship with Christ. All he wants to know is Christ, the power of His resurrection, and to share His life. He desires not to know **about** Christ, but to **personally** know Him.

What we see in this passage is that Paul passed over from a relationship based on law to one founded on intimate love. He passed from legalism to freedom. In every authentic relationship there is this passage, this leap, to a new level of consciousness.

As we reflect on this letter of Paul, we become aware that our human experience of love can discover its full potential within the intimacy of union with Christ.

SUGGESTED APPROACH TO PRAYER: DIALOGUE WITH CHRIST

+ Daily prayer pattern, pages 1 and 2.
     I quiet myself and relax in the presence of God.
     I declare my dependency on God.
+ Grace:
     I ask for the grace of freedom, i.e., for a readiness to respond with a clear "yes" to whatever I am called to by God, and a willingness to let go of all that is not in accordance with His values.
+ Method: It will be particularly helpful to read the explanation of journaling on pages 5 and 6.
     I will write a conversation with Jesus. I express fully my most profound sense of Him.
     I write His responses to me, allowing His spirit to address me through the written word.
     I close my prayer with an Our Father.
+ Review of Prayer:
     I write in my journal any feelings, experiences or insights that have come to my awareness during this prayer period.

ROMANS 8:18-25

> *I think that what we suffer in this life can never be*
> *compared to the glory, as yet unrevealed, which is*
> *waiting for us. The whole creation is eagerly waiting*
> *for God to reveal his sons. It was not for any fault*
> *on the part of creation that it was made unable to*
> *attain its purpose; it was made so by God; but creation*
> *still retains the hope of being freed, like us, from*
> *its slavery to decadence, to enjoy the same freedom and*
> *glory as the children of God. From the beginning till*
> *now the entire creation, as we know, has been groaning*
> *in one great act of giving birth, and not only creation,*
> *but all of us who possess the first fruits of the Spirit,*
> *we too groan inwardly as we wait for our bodies to be set*
> *free. For we must be content to hope that we shall be*
> *saved—our salvation is not in sight, we should not have*
> *to be hoping for it if it were—but, as I say, we must*
> *hope to be saved since we are not saved yet—it is*
> *something we must wait for with patience.*

COMMENTARY:

Just when we think the end is upon us, we discover it is the beginning! Just when we think our children are totally falling apart, we realize they are crossing over into adulthood.

Just when we think a friendship has totally collapsed, we become aware that it is being transformed from one of dependent need to one of mutual joy.

Just when we think a parish or congregation has become irrevocably fragmented, we see manifested within diverse views a bursting forth of a community based on authentic participatory leadership.

Just when we think our world is about to annihilate itself with nuclear weaponry, etc., we witness a rising awareness and responsiveness within a global networking of compassion.

To be authentically alive is to be in transition. It is to enter into the passages that mark our growth and development in wholeness.

In the letter of Paul, we are invited by God to midwife our own ongoing birth process! God presents us with challenges that demand all that we are, and blesses us with more than we dare dream.

We are challenged to be patient and to realize that within our own time and space we are, although broken and limited, moving toward the creation of a new age. Not just we but all of creation is being thrust forward into birth.

We are challenged to suffer while holding on to the belief that the suffering is a vital part of the transition toward new life.

We are challenged to eagerly expect that the inner reality and energy of the Spirit, though hidden, will be released and made visible . . . .

In the chaos of our lives, Paul—and Jesus—call us to hope. In hope is our freedom.

SUGGESTED APPROACH TO PRAYER: PRAYER OF HEALING

+ Daily prayer pattern, pages 1 and 2.
   I quiet myself and relax in the presence of God.
   I declare my dependency on God.
+ Grace:
   I ask for the grace of freedom, i.e., for a readiness to respond with a clear "yes" to whatever I am called to by God.
+ Method: Meditation, as on pages 2 and 3.
   I identify my deepest suffering or dis-ease at this time of my life.
   I listen to my wise mentor, Paul, speak his words to me in the words of the passage. As he speaks to me, I relate his words to my suffering. I listen deeply and open my pain to receive the healing energy of God's creative, hope-filled love.
   I close my prayer with an Our Father.
+ Review of Prayer:
   I write in my journal any feelings, experiences or insights that have come to my awareness during this prayer period.

80

SUGGESTED APPROACH TO PRAYER:

+ Daily prayer pattern, pages 1 and 2.

    I quiet myself and relax in the presence of God.

    I declare my dependency on God.

+ Grace:

    I ask for the grace of freedom, i.e., for a readiness to respond with a clear "yes" to whatever I am called to by God.

+ Method: Repetition, as on page 6.

    In preparation, I review my prayer by reading my journal of the past week. I select for my repetition the period of prayer in which I was most deeply moved by joy or gratitude or awe, or perhaps a passage that did not seem to touch me at all, or only painfully so. I proceed in the manner I did originally, opening my heart to this word of God.

+ Review of Prayer:

    I write in my journal any feelings, experiences or insights that have come to my awareness during this prayer period. I am particularly aware of how God may be gifting me with the grace I have been requesting.

ISAIAH 45:9-13

Can it argue with the man who fashioned it,
one vessel among earthen vessels?
Does the clay say to its fashioner, "What are you making?"
does the thing he shaped say, "You have no skill"?
Woe to him who says to a father, "What have you begotten?"
or to a woman, "To what have you given birth?"

Thus says Yahweh,
the Holy One, he who fashions Israel:
Is it for you to question me about my children
and to dictate to me what my hands should do?
I it was who made the earth,
and created man who is on it.
I it was who spread out the heavens with my hands
and now give orders to their whole array.
I it was who roused him to victory.
I leveled the way for him.
He will rebuild my city,
will bring my exiles back
without ransom or indemnity,
so says Yahweh Sabaoth.

COMMENTARY:

Primitive people recognized God in nature, not only in the tranquility and beauty but more dramatically in the unleashed power of wind, flood and fire.

Just as God is present in nature, He is present within our history. It seems, however, much easier to be in touch with the God of nature because to be in touch with the God of history requires reflection and a historical perspective.

No less dramatic than in nature are the forces and energies unleashed within human history. To "read" God's word in history demands a deep faith that God is present and active within the human situation.

In this passage from the book of Isaiah we are alerted to the great necessity there is for us to reflect upon and become astute at recognizing God's activity within world circumstances and historical events.

The historical circumstance emphasized in this passage is the hand and action of God in the appointment of Cyrus. Incredibly, Cyrus, a pagan, is an instrument of God in bringing about the reestablishment of Israel at the end of a long period of exile. The passage recalled for the Hebrew people God's faithfulness in the past and it served as a directive for them to sustain their confidence.

Unlike most cultures, the Hebrew people had an innate grasp of how God had been present to them within their history. This came primarily from a vivid recollection of their deliverance from Egyptian slavery. Their faith interpretation of the event was that God had directly intervened and led them to freedom across the Reed Sea.

In Yahweh, the God of history and the God of nature converged. The Hebrew people discovered that the God of history who delivered them was at once the God of nature who forged them creatively into a chosen people, a consecrated nation.

Our freedom is contingent upon our degree of belief and trust that God is just as present within the chaos—the fire, flood and wind—of contemporary events as He was present for the Hebrew people of ancient times. We, too, are to maintain confidence in Him. To surrender to His saving presence is to participate in the unfolding of His continuing creation.

SUGGESTED APPROACH TO PRAYER: PRAYING OVER OUR TIMES

+ Daily prayer pattern, pages 1 and 2.
    I quiet myself and relax in the presence of God.
    I declare my dependency on God.
+ Grace:
    I ask for the grace of freedom, i.e., for a readiness to see God's presence alive in our world.
+ Method:
    I prayerfully read the passage, letting the words find a home in me.
    I quietly page through a news magazine or newspaper. I read the

titles/headlines and look at the pictures with the eyes of faith. I intersperse my reflective perusal of the magazine or newspaper with a preferred line from the scripture passage, e.g., "It is I who made the earth" or "He will rebuild my city."

I close my prayer with an Our Father.

+ Review of Prayer:

I write in my journal any feelings, experiences or insights that have come to my awareness during this prayer period.

HEBREWS 11:17-19

> *It was by faith that Abraham, when put to the test,*
> *offered up Isaac. He offered to sacrifice his only*
> *son even though the promises had been made to him*
> *and he had been told: It is through Isaac that your*
> *name will be carried on. He was confident that God*
> *had the power even to raise the dead; and so, figuratively*
> *speaking, he was given back Isaac from the dead.*

COMMENTARY:

Have you ever had the experience of feeling that circumstances had put before you a task, work or project that seemed to integrate all factors of your life? Everything seemed to fit. The time was ripe. Perhaps it was to build a home, or begin a new career, to return to school, or to write a book. . . .

The direction seemed so clear that within your inner self you experienced it as God's intention for you. You claimed the task. You embraced the direction so deeply that it became, for you, the external expression of your personal relationship with God and his action through you.

You began. Obstacles arose, doors seemed closed. Tuition was more expensive than you imagined; career options were limited; there did not seem to be any interest in the subject you had chosen to write about!

In spite of the impediments, you continued to move ahead. You may have pulled back a bit, or slowed down, but you continued to plan and to work toward your goal.

You persevered because you believed in your dream. You believed that within yourself you had the gifts necessary. You believed that what you were doing would contribute significantly to something or someone beyond yourself.

In the face of the obstacles, you did not understand how this was going to be accomplished. It was not clear, but you went ahead.

This is faith.

Faith is an abstract word which, like love, has been overused to the point of having little content. For many people, faith is reduced to intellectual assent; for them faith never makes the journey from the head to the heart. Authentic faith resides most deeply in the heart.

One of the examples of faith that the author of Hebrews uses is Abraham's faith as expressed in his obedience to God when the death of his only son Isaac was demanded. Abraham did not comprehend why God would take away the life upon whom rested the promise of the future of the Israelite people. It did not make any sense!

Yet Abraham believed. His belief plunged him into the forces of darkness and death that paradoxically issued forth in new life.

Some things are constant: faith for us is what faith was for Abraham.

We, too, have our "Isaacs," those things or persons which are given and which we see as a means to some ultimate fulfillment. Only in surrendering them to God is the energy and power of new life released.

In the deliverance of Isaac, we find a symbol of the mystery of the death and resurrection of Jesus.

SUGGESTED APPROACH TO PRAYER: MEETING ISAAC

+ Daily prayer pattern, pages 1 and 2.

I quiet myself and relax in the presence of God.

I declare my dependency on God.

+ Grace:

I ask for the gift of freedom, i.e., a readiness to respond with a clear "yes" to whatever I am called to by God.

+ Method: Meditation, as on pages 2 and 3.

I ponder:

What is it that is most precious in my life? . . . a child? . . . a career? . . . a dream? . . . my health?

I see it before me as Abraham saw and embraced Isaac.

What is the worst thing that could happen?

I speak to God about "my Isaac." I tell Him what it means to me. I listen to hear what God will say to me about what it means to Him . . . what I mean to Him.

If I am able, I offer my Isaac to Him; I receive Isaac back from God.

If I am not able to offer my Isaac, I humbly beg for the desire.

I close my prayer with an Our Father.

+ Review of Prayer:

I write in my journal any feelings, experiences or insights that have come to my awareness during this prayer period.

I CORINTHIANS 9:19-23

> *So though I am not a slave of any man, I have made myself*
> *the slave of everyone so as to win as many as I could. I*
> *made myself a Jew to the Jews, to win the Jews; that is,*
> *I who am not a subject of the Law made myself a subject of*
> *the Law to those who are the subjects of the Law, to win*
> *those who are subject to the Law. To those who have no*
> *Law, I was free of the Law myself (though not free from*
> *God's Law, being under the law of Christ) to win those who*
> *have no Law. For the weak I made myself weak. I made*
> *myself all things to all men in order to save some at any*
> *cost; and I still do this, for the sake of the gospel, to*
> *have a share in its blessings.*

COMMENTARY:

"Side by side"—this phrase aptly describes Paul's way of sharing God's love. He becomes, as he said, *"all things to all people."*

This saying is often negated by the seemingly impossible demands it makes; it causes people to react with, "well, one can't be all things to all people."

This frequently results in a rationalization for "not being anything to anyone."

Paul is not suggesting that we **do** all things for all people. We are never to assume the responsibility either **of** others or **for** others.

Rather, he is speaking of his own inner attitude of adapting himself to the situation of others. This attitude flows from Paul's deep conviction that Christ reveals Himself to each person within each one's own particular circumstances.

Christ had grasped Paul so profoundly in his own life, that he was able to become confident and free enough to let go of the rigidities of the religious law of the Jews. No longer did the laws bind or control him; within the love of Christ he discovered their deeper meaning.

The original intent of the law was that it was meant to serve the people. It had become an absolute value unto itself.

For Paul, the absolute value within law would always be the love of Christ.

The ultimate worth of any value—personal, national or legal—is determined and judged by how well it serves and effects the law of love.

Being free within the law, Paul became a servant of love. He was able to communicate to those still bound by legalism, as well as those who rejected any law at all. His own freedom allowed him to move with ease and to accommodate the message to whomever he was addressing.

This "side by side" ministry serves as an example for our own ministry of love. What was required of Paul is required of us. Like Paul, we are to open ourselves to receive. We are to receive the love of God and to receive, within that love, all others.

Paul's voluntary submission to others, his "slavery," reflects the spirit of his Master, Jesus, who "emptied himself to assume the condition of a slave" (Phil. 2:7).

SUGGESTED APPROACH TO PRAYER: THE EYES OF JESUS

+ Daily prayer pattern, pages 1 and 2.
        I quiet myself and relax in the presence of God.
        I declare my dependency on God.
+ Grace:
        I ask for the grace of a radical openness before God.
+ Method: Centering prayer, as on pages 3 and 4.
        I see Jesus before me, looking at me.
        I allow Him to look at me lovingly . . . humbly.
        I realize that Jesus, in becoming human, became a servant of love.
        I open myself to receive His attention and care.
        I close my prayer with an Our Father.
+ Review of Prayer:
        I write in my journal any feelings, experiences or insights that have come to my awareness during this prayer period.

PHILIPPIANS 1:21-26

> *Life to me, of course, is Christ, but then death would*
> *bring me something more; but then again, if living in*
> *this body means doing work which is having good results—*
> *I do not know what I should choose. I am caught in this*
> *dilemma: I want to be gone and be with Christ, which*
> *would be very much the better, but for me to stay alive*
> *in this body is a more urgent need for your sake. This*
> *weighs with me so much that I feel sure I shall survive*
> *and stay with you all, and help you to progress in the*
> *faith and even increase your joy in it; and so you will*
> *have another reason to give praise to Christ Jesus on*
> *my account when I am with you again.*

COMMENTARY:

Paul wrote his beautiful and loving letter to the Philippian people from his prison cell.

For Paul, as for any Jew, to be in prison was to psychically encounter the issue of his own death. Imprisonment was an ancient symbol for death. The prison cell was frequently a windowless room with an opening in the ceiling through which the prisoner was dropped. It was the nearest thing to a tomb that one could imagine.

Here Paul awaited the trial that was likely to result in his death.

This letter bears the contemplative quality of one who had entered into his deepest self and found Christ.

Within this center he wrestled with the contradictions of life.

For Paul, to continue to live was, in a sense, to die, that is, to delay his complete union with Christ. On the other hand, for him to die would be ultimate life, in that he would at last arrive at total oneness with Christ.

He is in the dilemma between his own desires and the needs of those he loves and wants to bring to Christ. The weight is on the side of those he loves.

In the surrender of his own desire, as he places the matter of his life or death into the hands of God, Paul discovers the freedom of profound indifference.

What previously appeared contradictory is now resolved in the acceptance of paradox. Love has revealed and led the way to this resolution.

Paul arrives at the realization that to die or not to die is really not the question. The point of the entire argument is to be in Christ. While there surely is some advantage in death, he knows that being with and forming the Christian community is no less a union with Christ.

The beautiful prayer, "The Deer's Cry," might well be Paul's:

> *Christ with me, Christ before me, Christ behind me,*
> *Christ in me, Christ beneath me, Christ above me,*
> *Christ on my right, Christ on my left,*
> *Christ when I lie down, Christ when I sit down, Christ when*
> *   I arise,*
> *Christ in the heart of every one who thinks of me,*
> *Christ in the mouth of every one who speaks of me,*
> *Christ in every eye that sees me,*
> *Christ in every ear that hears me.*

SUGGESTED APPROACH TO PRAYER: DESCENT INTO PRISON

+ Daily prayer pattern, pages 1 and 2.

    I quiet myself and relax in the presence of God.

    I declare my dependency on God.

+ Grace:

    I ask for the grace of radical openness before God.

+ Method: Contemplation, as on page 3.

    I image myself being lowered into the prison with Paul. As I am lowered, I experience the depth of this prison. I gradually become aware of the darkness . . . and the cold dampness. My own feelings descend upon me . . . feelings of aloneness and of fear.

    I am aware that I am being chained. What are these chains? What are the contradictions that are holding me bound and imprisoned?

Are they anxieties about a long or short life, about health or sickness, riches or poverty, honor or dishonor?

I invite Jesus to be the resolution of whatever life dilemma I am presently experiencing.

I close my prayer by slowly praying, "The Deer's Cry."

+ Review of Prayer:

I write in my journal any feelings, experiences or insights that have come to my awareness during this prayer period.

SUGGESTED APPROACH TO PRAYER:

+ Daily prayer pattern, pages 1 and 2.
  I quiet myself and relax in the presence of God.
  I declare my dependency on God.
+ Grace:
  I ask God for the grace of a radical openness before God.
+ Method: Repetition, as on page 6.
  In preparation, I review my prayer by reading my journal of the past week. I select for my repetition the period of prayer in which I was most deeply moved by joy or gratitude or awe, or perhaps a passage that did not seem to speak to me at all, or only painfully so. I proceed in the manner suggested for that passage, opening my heart to hear the unique meaning of the Word of God for me.
+ Review of Prayer:
  I write in my journal any feelings, experiences or insights that have come to my awareness during this prayer period. I am particularly aware of how God may be gifting me with the grace I have been requesting.

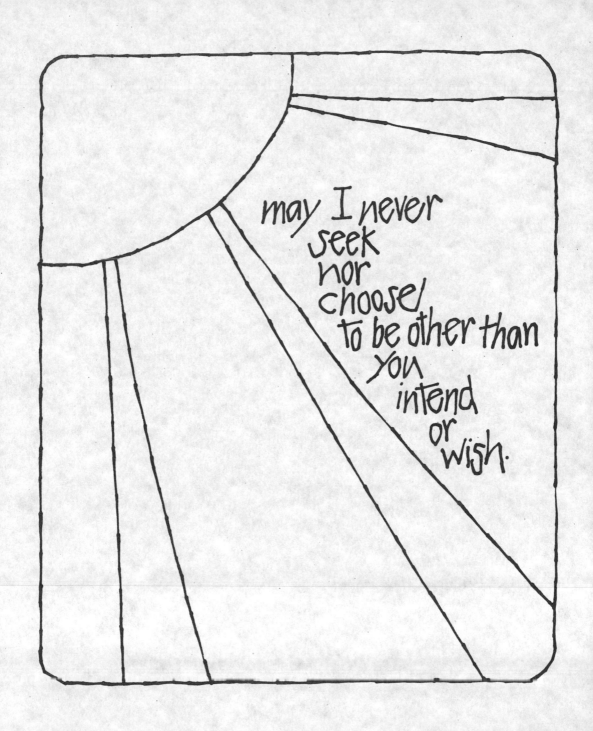

may I never
seek
nor
choose
to be other than
you
intend
or wish.

JOHN 3:22-32

After this, Jesus went with his disciples into the Judaean countryside and stayed with them there and baptized. At the same time John was baptizing at Aenon near Salim, where there was plenty of water, and people were going there to be baptized. This was before John had been put in prison.

Now some of John's disciples had opened a discussion with a Jew about purification, so they went to John and said, "Rabbi, the man who was with you on the far side of the Jordan, the man to whom you bore witness, is baptizing now, and everyone is going to him." John replied:

> *"A man can lay claim*
> *only to what is given him from heaven.*

"You yourselves can bear me out; I said: I myself am not the Christ; I am the one who has been sent in front of him.

> *"The bride is only for the bridegroom;*
> *and yet the bridegroom's friend,*
> *who stands there and listens,*
> *is glad when he hears the bridegroom's voice.*
> *This same joy I feel, and now it is complete.*
> *He must grow greater,*
> *I must grow smaller.*
> *He who comes from above*
> *is above all others;*
> *he who is born of the earth*
> *is earthly himself and speaks in an earthly way.*
> *He who comes from heaven*
> *bears witness to the things he has seen and heard,*
> *even if his testimony is not accepted . . . .*

COMMENTARY:

"Everyone is going to him" (v. 27).

This verse gives focus to the passage, which becomes clear as it unfolds.

The people are going to "him." They are drawn likes moths to light, like those who thirst are drawn to the spring.

The one they are drawn to is Jesus! He is the bridegroom!

The relationship between Jesus and John the Baptist receives beautiful expression within the rich imagery of oriental wedding customs. The use of marriage imagery recalls the covenant relationship between God and Israel, which was so close a bond that only the intimate union of marriage could begin to express it. In the Old Testament God is represented as a bridegroom and Israel is the bride.

In the New Testament Jesus is the bridegroom, the church is the bride, and John sees himself in the role of best man.

Under the canopy of Old Testament imagery each takes his/her proper role as God had ordained it.

Jesus the bridegroom. He is the central figure toward which everyone gravitates. He is not only the central figure of the New Testament, but He holds within His person, and is representative of, the collective consciousness of the entire Israelitic people.

In order to understand John's role, it is helpful to be aware of the role of best man in Jewish custom. As is customary even today, the man who is chosen as best man is usually the groom's best friend. In the time of Jesus, the honor of being chosen as best man was even more distinctive than it is now. He was the one in charge of arranging for the wedding, and presided as host at the feast. However, his most important responsibility was that of guarding the bridal chamber until the groom joined the bride. Only then were his duties completed.

John's task was to bring together Jesus and the community that John himself had nurtured and prepared for this moment. This is the same role that Moses had with respect to the Old Testament covenant between God and Israel. John, however, has even greater cause for joy and celebration. What Moses prophesied and foreshadowed has, through God's great love, been actualized. In Jesus, God has definitively embraced His people.

Having completed his task of preparing the way for Jesus, John withdraws.

98

He willingly, even joyfully, directs the attention away from himself to Jesus.

To anyone who would ask, John's reply might well have been:

> *I listen; he is the one that speaks;*
> *I am enlightened; he is the light;*
> *I am the ear; he is the word.* (St. Augustine)

I am the best man; Jesus is the bridegroom, and now is my "joy . . . complete" (v. 29).

SUGGESTED APPROACH TO PRAYER: IN HIS LIGHT

+ Daily prayer pattern, pages 1 and 2.

I quiet myself and relax in the presence of God.

I declare my dependency on God.

+ Grace:

I ask for the grace to desire to know and to do God's will, to commit myself to what is more for the greater honor and glory of God.

+ Method: Centering prayer, as on pages 3 and 4.

I see myself as a candle flame burning brightly. I have been burning for a long time and my flame is strong and casts a warm, beautiful glow.

Suddenly a brilliant light appears as if from a lighthouse. The light permeates and warms the entire space, spreading intense brightness.

I feel myself being absorbed by the light. My own flame seems to grow smaller and smaller until it is barely visible.

I relax in the glow; I allow myself to be embraced and held within its radiance.

I focus my heart on Jesus as Light, and very quietly repeat the name of Jesus.

I close my prayer with an Our Father.

+ Review of Prayer:

I write in my journal any feelings, experiences or insights that have come to my awareness during this prayer period.

I SAMUEL 3:1-11

Now the boy Samuel was ministering to Yahweh in the presence of Eli; it was rare for Yahweh to speak in those days; visions were uncommon. One day, it happened that Eli was lying down in his room. His eyes were beginning to grow dim; he could no longer see. The lamp of God had not yet gone out, and Samuel was lying in the sanctuary of Yahweh where the ark of God was, when Yahweh called, "Samuel! Samuel!" He answered, "Here I am." Then he ran to Eli and said, "Here I am, since you called me." Eli said, "I did not call. Go back and lie down." So he went and lay down. Once again Yahweh called, "Samuel! Samuel!" Samuel got up and went to Eli and said, "Here I am, since you called me." He replied, "I did not call you, my son; go back and lie down." Samuel had as yet no knowledge of Yahweh and the word of Yahweh had not yet been revealed to him. Once again Yahweh called, the third time. He got up and went to Eli and said, "Here I am, since you called me." Eli then understood that it was Yahweh who was calling the boy, and he said to Samuel, "Go, and lie down, and if someone calls, say, 'Speak, Yahweh, your servant is listening'." So Samuel went and lay down in his place.

Yahweh then came and stood by, calling as he had done before, "Samuel! Samuel!" Samuel answered, "Speak, Yahweh, your servant is listening." Then Yahweh said to Samuel, "I am about to do such a thing in Israel as will make the ears of all who hear it ring."

COMMENTARY:

God speaks sometimes in the gentle breeze . . . sometimes in the quiet of night . . . sometimes within our child heart. In prayer, we hear our name called.

This was Samuel's experience, just as it was the experience of the prophets who preceded him, Abraham, Jacob and Moses. Samuel responded with the same words and the same total generosity and openness. *"Here I am, Lord."*

Each of us has an inner voice, a voice which calls us to be who we are. To be who we are is an "election" by God. To embrace the unique "word" God speaks in creating us, in calling us by name, is to encounter God.

To say, "Here I am, Lord," is to have the audacity to believe in and the courage to exercise the particular gifts that identify one's deepest self.

One of the greatest temptations is to doubt our own experience of God. Eventually, we, too, may need an Eli—a representative of the community—with whom to test the spirit.

Meanwhile, we, like Samuel, need to enter the night . . . to rest . . . to listen for the moment when God speaks our name.

SUGGESTED APPROACH TO PRAYER: GOD SPEAKS MY NAME

+ Daily prayer pattern, pages 1 and 2.
>   I quiet myself and relax in the presence of God.
>   I declare my dependency on God.

+ Grace:
>   I ask for the grace to desire to know and to do God's will, to commit myself to what is more for the greater glory and honor of God.

+ Method: Contemplation, as on page 3.
>   I enter into a state of profound relaxation, nearly asleep. As Samuel did, I hear God speak my name, " _____."
>   By what name does God call me—my full baptismal name? . . . my nickname? . . . by a term of endearment? . . . or . . . ?
>   What is the tenor of God's voice as He speaks my name? Is it urgent, or gentle, or begging, or . . . ?
>   I open myself to receive his call.
>   I let my heart respond.
>   I close my prayer with an Our Father.

+ Review of Prayer:
>   I write in my journal any feelings, experiences or insights that have come to my awareness during this prayer period.

LUKE 1:26-38

> *In the sixth month the angel Gabriel was sent by God to*
> *a town in Galilee called Nazareth, to a virgin betrothed*
> *to a man named Joseph, of the House of David; and the*
> *virgin's name was Mary. He went in and said to her,*
> *"Rejoice, so highly favored! The Lord is with you." She*
> *was deeply disturbed by these words and asked herself*
> *what this greeting could mean, but the angel said to her,*
> *"Mary, do not be afraid; you have won God's favor.*
> *Listen! You are to conceive and bear a son, and you must*
> *name him Jesus. He will be great and will be called Son*
> *of the Most High. The Lord God will give him the throne*
> *of his ancestor David; he will rule over the House of Jacob*
> *for ever and his reign will have no end." Mary said to the*
> *angel, "But how can this come about, since I am a virgin?"*
> *"The Holy Spirit will come upon you," the angel answered,*
> *"and the power of the Most High will cover you with its*
> *shadow. And so the child will be holy and will be called*
> *Son of God. Know this too: your kinswoman Elizabeth has,*
> *in her old age, conceived a son, and she whom people called*
> *barren is now in her sixth month, for nothing is impossible*
> *to God." "I am the handmaid of the Lord," said Mary, "let*
> *what you have said be done to me." And the angel left her.*

COMMENTARY:

"Let what you have said be done to me."

This response of Mary to the angelic announcement of the birth of Jesus paints for us the portrait of Mary as the first Christian disciple.

It has been suggested that, in writing this passage, Luke drew on what he knew of Mary in her later ministry.

We know that Jesus praised His mother as one of those who heard the word of God and put it into practice. (Lk. 8:21) She was a woman obedient to the word of God.

At the moment of Mary's willing response to God's action in her life, all the hopes of humanity were realized. She is the convergent point of the two covenants. In her, the covenant of God with Israel gave way to the emergence of the covenant of Christ with His Church. Mary is, therefore, the mother of the Church. The Word of God was conceived within her; and in the Word all things are conceived.

What every follower of Jesus is called to do, Mary did first. She exemplified what we read in John 12:24: *"Unless the grain of wheat falls on the ground and dies, it remains alone; but if it dies, it yields a rich harvest."*

In Mary's total yielding of self, we recognize the same spirit of total surrender to the Father that characterized the final cry of her Son, *"Into your hands I commend my spirit"* (Lk. 23:46).

SUGGESTED APPROACH TO PRAYER: WITH MARY

+ Daily prayer pattern, pages 1 and 2.
> I quiet myself and relax in the presence of God.
> I declare my dependency on God.
+ Grace:
> I ask for the grace to desire to know and to do God's will, and to commit myself to what is more for the glory of God.
+ Method: Contemplation, as on page 3.
> I image myself as Mary. I use the passage as a script to enter into the unfolding drama of the Annunciation.
> I picture myself in the home of Mary, suddenly startled by the visit of an angel.
> I allow myself to be opened to her experience of surprise . . . fear . . . confusion . . . amazement, and ultimately, to her generosity of response.
> With Mary, I, too, yield to God's inviting word and spirit within my heart.
> I close my prayer with an Our Father.
+ Review of Prayer:
> I write in my journal any feelings, experiences or insights that have come to my awareness during this prayer period.

WISDOM 9:1-12

"God of our ancestors, Lord of mercy,
who by your word have made all things,
and in your wisdom have fitted man
to rule the creatures that have come from you,
to govern the world in holiness and justice
and in honesty of soul to wield authority,
grant me Wisdom, consort of your throne,
and do not reject me from the number of your children.

"For I am your servant, son of your serving maid,
a feeble man, with little time to live,
with small understanding of justice and the laws.
Indeed, were anyone perfect among the sons of men,
if he lacked the Wisdom that comes from you, he would still
     count for nothing.
You yourself have chosen me to be king over your people,
to be judge of your sons and daughters.
You have bidden me build a temple on your holy mountain,
an altar in the city where you have pitched your tent,
a copy of that sacred tabernacle which you prepared
     from the beginning.
With you is Wisdom, she who knows your works,
she who was present when you made the world;
she understands what is pleasing in your eyes
and what agrees with your commandments.
Dispatch her from the holy heavens,
send her forth from your throne of glory
to help me and to toil with me
and teach me what is pleasing to you,
since she knows and understands everything.
She will guide me prudently in my undertakings

and protect me by her glory.
Then all I do will be acceptable,
I shall govern your people justly
and shall be worthy of my father's throne.

COMMENTARY:

"Watch for her early . . . you'll find her sitting at your gates" (Wisdom 6:11). She will be your friend (1:6). When she is your friend, all good things will come to you (7:11). Her radiance will not sleep (7:10), and she will be for you an inexhaustible treasure (7:15). Through her you will become friends with God (7:14).

She is a beautiful woman (Prov. 8:1-21) and mirrors God's own goodness (Ws. 7:26). She will be your comfort and your counselor (8:9).

Pray, and she will come to you (7:7).

Her name is Wisdom.

In the Old Testament wisdom literature, wisdom is represented as a woman. As the feminine dimension of God's power, wisdom is seen as accompanying Yahweh in His creation (Pr. 8:22-31).

To receive the gift of wisdom from God is to have the knowledge and skill to respond to life situations and problems with ease. It is to be able to encounter life within a framework of balance and in a realistic, practical and moral manner. Through this gift of discernment we become partners with God in His ongoing creation.

Wisdom 9:1-12 is a prayer, placed on the lips of the king, asking for wisdom.

SUGGESTED APPROACH TO PRAYER: TO SPEAK WITH WISDOM

+ Daily prayer pattern, pages 1 and 2.
   I quiet myself and relax in the presence of God.
   I declare my dependency on God.
+ Grace:
   I ask for the gift that all my desires will be ordered to the fulfillment of God's plan and wisdom.
+ Method: Journaling, as on page 5.
   I see Wisdom as a person. I image her. What does she look like?

—old, young?

—how is she dressed?

. . . what do I know of her?

—where does she live?

—how far has she traveled?

—what are her experiences?

. . . what has been my relationship with her?

—in the past?

—now?

I enter into a written conversation with Wisdom.

She speaks to me; I respond to her.

I relax and let the words flow freely from my pen.

I reverently reread the passage.

I conclude my prayer with the Our Father.

+ Review of Prayer:

I write in my journal any feelings, experiences or insights that have come to my awareness during this prayer period.

ROMANS 8:31-39

After saying this, what can we add? With God on our side
who can be against us? Since God did not spare his own Son,
but gave him up to benefit us all, we may be certain, after
such a gift, that he will not refuse anything he can give.
Could anyone accuse those that God has chosen? When God
acquits, could anyone condemn? Could Christ Jesus? No!
He not only died for us—he rose from the dead, and there
at God's right hand he stands and pleads for us.

Nothing therefore can come between us and the love of Christ,
even if we are troubled or worried, or being persecuted, or
lacking food or clothes, or being threatened or even attacked.
As scripture promised: For your sake we are being massacred
daily and reckoned as sheep for the slaughter. These are
the trials through which we triumph, by the power of him
who loved us.

For I am certain of this: neither death nor life, no angel,
no prince, nothing that exists, nothing still to come, not any
power, or height or depth, nor any created thing, can ever
come between us and the love of God made visible in Christ
Jesus our Lord.

COMMENTARY:

"We the jury find the defendant not guilty as charged."

This courtroom acquittal precipitates immense relief and joy for those who have been brought to the court of justice. With these words one has been found innocent and freed.

Our heart, too, can rejoice. Our "judgment" has already taken place. We, too, have been pronounced "not guilty." We have been found innocent and are freed.

This amazing announcement is the underlying conviction within the hymn of love found in Paul's letter written to the Romans.

The significance of the passage lies in its being the bridge for us from our image of Christ as judge to one of Christ as lover.

In verses 31-35, we are assured that God is on our side and has acquitted us.

Can anyone condemn us? If anyone could, or would have the right, it would be Jesus.

Jesus knows how much we sin because by His sufferings He has taken our faults on Himself.

Jesus does not act, however, as our judge.

Though Jesus pleads our cause, it is not as a trial attorney, but rather it is out of deep love. He stands as One who will be heard, at the Father's right hand, appealing to God to grant us innocence, that is, freedom. It is the freedom to love and to receive love.

In Jesus, God's love is translated into human terms. *"He is the image of the unseen God and the firstborn of all creation.* (Col. 1:15).

We have been thought of and loved by God with the same thought and love He had for His Son. We, too, have been created in His image (Gn. 1:27). We are sons and daughters of God and as such are to respond to God with love, the love that originated with God, for *"He first loved us"* (I Jn. 4:19).

In other words, the love is of God. It is the essence, the very breath of our existence. Therefore, we cannot possibly be separated from love, from God.

Our union with Jesus expresses the fullness of that love. Temptation or suffering cannot rob us of it, but can only draw us deeper into love. In some mysterious way, our sufferings and temptations, even though hidden, are part of Jesus' own suffering and temptation.

We are loved! Can He who did not spare His own Son for our sake refuse us anything?

SUGGESTED APPROACH TO PRAYER: CONVERSATION WITH JESUS

+ Daily prayer pattern, pages 1 and 2.
    I quiet myself and relax in the presence of God.
    I declare my dependency on God.

+ Grace:
   I ask for the gift of experiencing deeply the love of Jesus for me.
+ Method: Contemplation, as on page 3.
   I imagine Jesus sitting close to me. He is present to me as a friend who loves me.
   I speak to Him. I tell Him of my deepest desire . . . of my greatest joys and most profound fears . . . .
   If there is no one else around, I speak aloud.
   I listen to what He says to me, i.e., I pause frequently to listen to what Jesus wishes to express to me within my heart.
   As the conversation concludes, I repeat the name of Jesus, over and over, slowly, quietly.
   I pray the Our Father with Jesus.
+ Review of Prayer:
   I write in my journal any feelings, experiences or insights that have come to my awareness during this prayer period.

EPHESIANS 3:14-21

This, then, is what I pray, kneeling before the Father
from whom every family, whether spiritual or natural,
takes its name:

Out of his infinite glory, may he give you the power
through his Spirit for your hidden self to grow strong,
so that Christ may live in your hearts through faith,
and then, planted in love and built on love, you will
with all the saints have strength to grasp the breadth
and the length, the height and the depth; until, knowing
the love of Christ, which is beyond all knowledge, you
are filled with the utter fullness of God.

Glory be to him whose power, working in us, can do infinitely
more than we can ask or imagine; glory be to him
from generation to generation in the Church and in Christ
Jesus for ever and ever. Amen.

COMMENTARY:

Do you remember ever unexpectedly coming upon your mother or father while they were at prayer? You may have become aware of a quiet gentleness of expression, or even of tears. It was as if you had entered into a hidden, sacred space.

Reading this passage is somewhat like coming upon Paul while he is at prayer. He reveals to us his deep love of Christ and his concern for the church. His own personal struggle is also reflected in his prayer.

Paul is kneeling; Jews usually stood to pray. To kneel while praying was more characteristic of pagans. Paul may have assumed this form as a way of expressing his hope for the eventual union of Jews and Gentiles. It may well have been an ecumenical gesture. Or, it may simply have been, for him, a spontaneous act which was precipitated by the intensity of his prayer.

In the prayer, Paul places himself before the Father. The intimate tone of the passage tells us something of Paul's relationship with God, it was as a son to his father.

With the birth of Christianity, the fatherhood of God came to be seen as one which offered total accessibility and intimacy to all. This differed from the previous understanding that tended to restrict the fatherhood of the gods exclusively to the act of creation, and therefore limited God's accessibility and intimacy.

Paul's prayer is a prayer for wholeness. His world was much like our own. It was an age of transition characterized by the death of the old and the not-yet-realized birth of the new. Many of the systems: political, social, economic and religious, were no longer viable or effective. It was a scenario of collapse and chaos.

Then, as now, what was occurring in the larger world was also taking place within individuals. As they struggled with the chaos that existed within themselves, they wrestled with the questions of: Who am I? . . . a broken person in a broken world? Where is my hope?

Paul knew brokenness. He was no stranger to the inner struggle. Under the impact of his meeting with Christ on the road to Damascus (Acts 9), he experienced his personal fragmentation when the egocentric strivings, in which his personal identity was invested, collapsed.

Paul knew hope. He discovered that the wholeness of Jesus was what gave his life meaning. That is why he prays so fervently that the "hidden self" of his disciples would grow strong in, with and through Christ.

Paul closes his prayer with praise to God for the transforming power that is God's gift to all who believe in Jesus. It is through this energizing Spirit of love that Jesus unites His followers, however broken, and brings to fulfillment His presence in His Body, the Church.

SUGGESTED APPROACH TO PRAYER: PRAYING WITH PAUL

+ Daily prayer pattern, pages 1 and 2.
    I quiet myself and relax in the presence of God.
    I declare my dependency on God.

+ Grace:

I ask for the grace to open my heart and to receive God's love deeply, trustingly.

+ Method: Meditation, as on page 2

I let my heart pray this passage for my deepest self. It is Paul's prayer for me; it is the desire that Christ has for me. I let my heart respond.

I will repeat reflectively the phrase that I find speaks most directly to where I experience need.

I will pause and savor those phrases which I find most consoling and most encouraging.

I close my prayer with an Our Father.

+ Review of Prayer:

I write in my journal any feelings, experiences or insights that have come to my awareness during this prayer period.

SUGGESTED APPROACH TO PRAYER:

+ Daily prayer pattern, pages 1 and 2.
    I quiet myself and relax in the presence of God.
    I declare my dependency on God.
+ Grace:
    I ask for the grace of profound thankfulness for the gift of God's love.
    Method: Repetition, as on pages 5 and 6, and Journaling as on page 5.
    During several prayer periods I reread my prayer journal of the past weeks. I become aware of how my prayer and the events of my life have mutually influenced each other in the course of this time.
    God has spoken to me, in love, during these past weeks.
    I use a prayer period to respond to His love by writing a letter to God. I let my heart speak.

Appendices

FOR SPIRITUAL DIRECTORS

The passages and commentaries are keyed to the basic movements of the Principle and Foundation as it is found in the SPIRITUAL EXERCISES OF ST. IGNATIUS.

FOR SPIRITUAL DIRECTORS, Continued

COMMITMENT/MAGIS—May I never seek to be other than you intend

INDEX OF APPROACHES TO PRAYER

INDEX OF APPROACHES TO PRAYER, Continued

COMMITMENT:

Index of Scripture Passages

*Page numbers preceded by a bold *B* are in *Birth: A Guide for Prayer*, Take and Receive series.
**Page numbers preceded by a bold *F* are in *Forgiveness: A Guide for Prayer*, Take and Receive series.
***Page numbers preceded by a bold *L* are in *Love: A Guide for Prayer*, Take and Receive series.

BIBLIOGRAPHY

1. Anderson, Bernard W. *Understanding the Old Testament*. Englewood Cliffs, NJ: Prentice-Hall, 1975.
2. Barclay, William. *The Daily Study Bible Series*. Philadelphia: Westminster Press, 1975.
3. Barth, Karl. *A Shorter Commentary on Romans*. Richmond: John Knox Press, 1963.
4. Bridges, Robert, ed. *Poems of Gerard Manley Hopkins*. New York: Oxford University Press, 1948.
5. Bright, John. *Jeremiah*. Garden City, NY: Doubleday & Co., 1965.
6. Brown, Raymond E. *The Birth of the Messiah*. Garden City, NY: Image Books, 1979.
7. _____. *The Gospel According to John I-XII*. Garden City, NY: Doubleday & Co., 1966.
8. _____, et al. *The Jerome Biblical Commentary*. Englewood Cliffs, NJ: Prentice-Hall, 1968.
9. Caird, G. B. *Saint Luke*. London: Penguin Books, 1963.
10. Cowan, Marian, and John C. Futrell. *The Spiritual Exercises of St. Ignatius of Loyola: A Handbook for Directors*. New York: Le Jacq Publishing, 1982.
11. Dahood, Mitchell. *Psalms I, II, III*. Garden City, NY: Doubleday & Co., 1966, 1968, 1970.
12. de Mello, Anthony. *Sadhana, A Way to God*. Saint Louis: The Institute of Jesuit Sources, 1978.
13. English, John. *Spiritual Freedom*. Guelph, Ontario: Loyola House, 1974.
14. Ferrucci, Piero. *What We May Be*. Los Angeles: J. P. Tarcher, 1982.
15. Fitzmeyer, Joseph. *The Gospel According to Luke I-IX*. Garden City, NY: Doubleday & Co., 1981.
16. Fleming, David. *The Spiritual Exercises of St. Ignatius: A Literal Translation and a Contemporary Reading*. Saint Louis: The Institute of Jesuit Sources, 1978.
17. Heschel, Abraham J. *The Prophets*. New York: Harper & Row, Publishers, 1962.
18. Jung, Carl G. *Man and His Symbols.* New York: Valor Publications, 1964.

18. Jung, Carl G. *Man and His Symbols*. New York: Valor Publications, 1964.

19. Leslie, Elmer A. *The Psalms*. New York: Abingdon Press, 1949.

20. Magaña, José, S.J. *A Strategy for Liberation*. Hicksville, NY: Exposition Press, 1974.

21. Maloney, George A., S. J. *Prayer of the Heart*. Notre Dame, IN: Ave Maria Press, 1981.

22. McKenzie, John. *Second Isaiah*. Garden City, NY: Doubleday & Co., Inc., 1968.

23. _____. *Dictionary of the Bible*. Milwaukee: The Bruce Publishing Co., 1965.

24. Orr, William and James Arthur Walther. *I Corinthians*. Garden City, NY: Doubleday & Co., Inc., 1976.

25. Pennington, M. Basil. *Centering Prayer*. Garden City, NY: Image Books, 1982.

26. Pope, Marvin H. *Job*. Garden City, NY: Doubleday & Co., Inc., 1965.

27. Rahner, Karl. *Spiritual Exercises*. New York: Herder and Herder, 1956.

28. Simons, George F. *Journal for Life, Part One: Foundations*. Chicago: ACTA, 1975.

29. Speiser, E. A. *Genesis*. Garden City, NY: Doubleday & Co., Inc., 1964.

30. Thompson, Francis. *The Hound of Heaven*. New York: Dodd, Mead and Co., 1963.

31. Veltri, John, S.J. *Orientations, Vol. I: A Collection of Helps for Prayer*. Guelph, Ontario: Loyola House, 1979.

32. _____. *Orientations, Vol. II: Annotation 19: Tentative Edition*. Guelph, Ontario: Loyola House, 1981.

TO OUR READERS:

It would be helpful to us, as we prepare to write the subsequent volumes of this series of guides for prayer, if you would be willing to respond to the following questions, and send your response to us.

Thank you.

Jacqueline
Marie

— —

Check appropriate answers; give comments.

1. I used the guide for prayer
   _____ regularly over a period of _____ (weeks / months).
   _____ irregularly.
   Comment:

2. I found the format, i.e., cover design, paper, layout
   _____ helpful to my prayer.
   Comment:

3. I found the commentaries
   _____ helpful for entering into prayer.
   _____ difficult to understand.
   Comment:

4. The commentaries that were most helpful were on pages _____
   _____

5. I (used / did not use) the approaches to prayer.
   Comment:

6. What I liked best about the guide for prayer is: _____
   _____
   _____

7. The following changes or additions would make the guide for prayer more
   helpful _____
   _____
   _____

   _____
   Signature optional

Mail to: Center for Christian Renewal, Box 87, Crookston, MN 56716